THE
Goals

SUHEIR AL HASAN

authorHOUSE

AuthorHouse™
1663 Liberty Drive
Bloomington, IN 47403
www.authorhouse.com
Phone: 833-262-8899

Published by AuthorHouse 08/05/2020

ISBN: 978-1-7283-6785-9 (sc)
ISBN: 978-1-7283-6981-5 (e)

Print information available on the last page.

Any people depicted in stock imagery provided by Getty Images are models, and such images are being used for illustrative purposes only.
Certain stock imagery © Getty Images.

This book is printed on acid-free paper.

Special thanks to my beloved husband who
Stood by my side throughout my work with this book

شـكر خاص الى زوجـــي الغــالي الذي ساندني و وقف بجانبي
طوال فترة انشغالي بكتابة هذا الكتاب

CONTENTS

المــــتويات

INTRODUCTION

May God's peace, mercy, and blessings be upon you
Then .. This Book Is a Dedicated to Each One Who Have Merit Over Me, Especially My Parents, May Allah Reward Them For What They Did For me ..
And To The One Who Taught Us The Morality, And to The One Who brighten the darkness of our minds with the light of knowledge and sincerity, And progress
And prosperity, To our beloved Al Mustafa Muhammad Peace Be Upon Him, May Allah reward our Prophet Muhammad, the best of reward of
A prophet on his Ummah
All The Effort Which Spend On This Book And More Than It, Is Summary And Explaining Saying For Our Prophet Mohammed Peace Be Upon Him Which Is Says (The Deeds Counts By Its Intention, And Each One Will Reward As What He Intent)
Peace Be Upon Who Was Meaningfully In His Saying And The Accomplishments With Purposes And Goals In His Deeds ..
Peace Be Upon You Oh Or Prophet The Messenger Of God
Oh God, Make Our Work Sincere For You
And make it an argument for us, not on us, Oh Our Lord Make This Book Useful For Our Nation .. And Each Mistake Is From Myself So Excuse Me.. Some People Will See This Book Is Too serious .. Or Sometimes Need To Be More serious In Another Point, But I meant That The Goals And The noble intention, The Planning .. The Hard Work, Can Be In a Very Simple Things In Our Life ..You Don't Have To Change The World Just Because You Have a Matter Or Goal .. But Maybe You Have One Goal Which Is Make Your Parents Happy Is One Of The Most Noble Goal You Can Work For ..So Simplify ... It Is Like a Calling For Simplicity And Returning For a Goodness That You Can Do Your Best To Share Love And Goodness .. Peace Be Upon Him Says Your Smiling With Your Brother Is charity .And You Have To Know That Not Everything You Plan For You Can Get It .. Do Your BestAnd Let The Rest For Our Lord ..
So You May Do Your Best And Spend Your Effort .. And You'll Get Nothing .. For Reason No One Can Know Except Our Lord .. So Never Give Up ..
Be Patient.. Because Each High Ambition And Each Special Goal Have Some Obstacles. You Have Real Intention Then You'll Get Your Target .
So Keep Your Intention ..
Oh Allah Forgive Us Our slips And Accept It From Us ... Oh Our Lord Make Us From Those Who benefited from the blessings of your Prophet's words Peace Be Upon Him

.. Enjoy The Reading And Good Luck

مـــقـــدمـــة

السلام عليكم ورحمة الله وبركاته

اما بعد ... هذا الكتاب هو إهداء الى كل من له فضل عليَّ ..ومنهم بالاخص والديَّ .. جزاهم الله عني خير ماجزى والد عن ولده

والى من علمنا الاخلاق .. والى من أنار ظلام عقولنا بنور العلم والاخلاص .. والتقدم والازدهار ... الى حضرة حبيبنا المصطفى محمد ﷺ جزى الله عنا نبينا محمد خير ماجزى نبي عن امته ..

عسى الله ان يتقبل منّا ... اللهم جِئْنَاكَ بِبِضَاعَةٍ مُزْجَاةٍ فَأَوْفِ لَنَا الْكَيْلَ وَتَصَدَّقْ عَلَيْنَا ..

كل الجهد المبذول في هذا الكتاب وأكثر من ذلك هو خلاصة ويدور بمداره حول قوله ﷺ {إنما الأعمال بالنيات، وإنما لكل امرئ ما نوى } صلى الله على من كان البلاغة والفصاحة في قوله .. والانجاز والغايات في عمله

صلى الله عليك ياسيدي يارسول الله .. اللهم اجعل عملنا خالصاً لوجهك الكريم واجعله حجة لنا لا علينا برحمتك ياارحم الراحمين ... اللهم نفع بكتابي هذا أمة حبيبك المصطفى ﷺ.. وكل تقصير وزلل فهو من نفسي .. فالتمسوا لي العذر

وقد يرى البعض في هذا الكتاب شئ من الجدية المفرطة احياناً او شئ من التفريط احياناً ولكني قصدت بذلك ان ينتبه القراء الى ان الاهداف والتخطيط والنية النبيلة قد تكون بابسط الاسباب وبابسط الاشياء والافعال

انت لايجب ان تغير الكون او العالم لتكون لديك هدف هدفك قد يكون هدفك ادخال البهجة على والدك و هذا من اعظم الاعمال لذلك.. بسِّـــــــط .. هي دعوة للبساطة والسهولة .. وعودة للفطرة النقية التي تميل الى فعل الخير مهما كان بسيطاً ..

فتبسمك بوجه اخيك صدقة صلى الله على من علمنا ذلك ...

كذلك أُنبه الى ان ليس كل مايريد المرء يدركه فاذا عزمت فتوكل على الله ودائما قل إن شاء الله ... والحقيقة انه لايتحرك متحرك إلا باذن الله .. فلنعلم ذلك

فقد تفعل كل الصواب وتبذل كل الجهد .. ولاتحصل على شئ .. اللهم لا يفع ذا الجد منك الجد يا اللــــه

فلتكن صبورا على غايتك ... تمسك بهمتك .. والتمس البساطة في خطواتك فكل همة عالية وكل نية صادقة وكل غاية نبيلة تتحقق ولكن قد تكون هناك بعض العقبات .. هذه العقبات هي لغاية يعلمها الله

اللهم اغفر لنا زلاتنا .. وتقبل منا ... وانفعنا ببركة كلام نبيك المصطفى صلوات ربي وسلامه عليه

اللـــــهم هذا الدعـــــاء ومنك الاجـــابة .. وهـــذا الجهد وعليك التكلان

اتمنى لكم قراءة ممتعة

وشـــــكراً لـــــكم

SECTION 1
ABOUT THE GOALS

الفصـــل الأول
ماهيـــة الأهـــداف

1-WHAT IS THE GOALS MEAN:-

Many people wonder what is my goal?. Why do I need to set a goal.. When I can live my life smoothly simply without setting any goal? Why I have to carry a heavy bag?

Question:-

What is your goal?

. (My goal is to become a doctor . . . or a teacher ...or ... veterinary. Etc.)

And that answer could be correct. And for real these are beautiful targets. But they are long-term targets. These targets can be lost easily

So to understand the answer

Your goal now is your need now. What do you need now? Determine your need now. And make it the target. Like,

I want to have my own room. Or my own corner in the home ... I want to set it as I want. ... So that's your goal at this moment.

I want to have the first hour of the morning, specific for me. To study, to meditate, or to pray. That's your goal for right now.

If you can own your room... Or your place in the home... And you can set it as you want so this can be accomplish for you ...

And you can feel that you are happy to get it by yourself.

If you can have the first hour in the morning just for yourself... Away from hassle and responsibilities so you already got your goal.

And you can be happy for that.

So its small goals but still its goals... And when you get it... It's can make you happy

Because if you don't have a small goals you can live randomly.

And you can be boredom

.

If you faced yourself in the mirror... And faced the truth as it is. I want to be a doctor, an engineer or a veterinarian,

It wasn't a (needs) as much as a (wishes)... and you know wishes could be or could not be achieved, but the goal is something you want at this moment and you working for it,

So decide what you want for right now!

Meaning deep and easy

1- ماهية الاهداف

السلام عليكم ورحمه الله وبركاته

الكثير يتساءل ماهو هدفي .. ولماذا تكلموني عن الأهداف ... لماذا تحملني حقيبه ثقيله..(هدفي هو أن أصبح طبيب أو معلم .. أو بيطري ... الخ)

وهذه الاجابة قد تكون صحيحة .. وفعلا هذه اهداف جميلة .. ولكنها اهداف على المدى البعيد .. وهذه الاهداف معرضة للضياع بسهولة ..

لكي تفهم الإجابه

هدفك الان هو احتياجك الان .. ماهو احتياجك الان .. حدد احتياجك الان .. واجعله الهدف .. مثلا اريد ان يكون لي غرفتي الخاصة .. او ركني الخاص ... ارتبه كيفما اريد . ... اذن هذا هو هدفك في هذه اللحظة .

اريد ان يكون لي الساعة الاولى من الصباح خاصة لي .. للدراسة او للتامل او للصلاة .. هذا هو هدفك الان

إذا كان يمكنك امتلاك غرفتك... أو مكانك في المنزل... ويمكنك ترتيبه كما تريد هذا يمكن ان يكون إنجاز لك... ويمكنك ان تشعر انك سعيد للحصول عليه.

إذا كان يمكنك الحصول علي الساعة الاولي في الصباح فقط لنفسك... بعيدا عن المتاعب والمسؤوليات فانت بالفعل حصلت علي هدفك. ويمكنك ان تكون سعيدا لذلك. لذلك هي اهداف صغيرة ولكنها لا تزال أهداف.. وعندما تحصل عليها... يمكن ان تجعلك سعيدا لأنه إذا لم يكن لديك أهداف صغيره يمكنك العيش بشكل عشوائي.عندها يمكن ان تكون ضجرا.

لو واجهت نفسك بالمرآة ... وواجهت الحقيقه كما هي لوجدت أن

إذن ! فاجابتك اريد ان اكون طبيب او مهندس او بيطري هي لم تكن حاجة بقدر ماهي امنية ... قد تتحقق او قد لاتتحقق

4

The goal here is related to your needs..... How do you want to live ... At any level ... By any way ... What do you want now?

The more you can fix your environment (house ... room ... yard ... car ... work .... Losing weight .... Etc.) to be at your level that satisfies your desire. Mean you can be yourself then you can get your goal,

When I asked you about it, you answered me with answers far away from you... These answers are answers to another question that may be (one day what do you wish to be?) Then you can answer me (doctor ... or minister ... Or an engineer).

اما الهدف فهو حاجة انت تريدها في هذه اللحظة وتعمل لاجلها

اذن حدد ماذا تريد الآن ؟! ..

معنى مع سهولته عميق .. ومفهوم قد يغير ميزانك للأشياء .كلياً ..

طيب مادخل هذه المقدمه بسؤالك

(ما هــــو هدفـــــــك ؟!.)

الهدف هنا متعلق بإحتياجك ..... كيف تريد أن تعيش ... بأي مستوى ... بأي طريقه ... ماذا تريد الآن ؟

كلما إستطعت أن تصلح بيئتك لتكون بالمستوى اللائق بك بالمستوى الذي يشبع رغبتك .. حاجتك .. تكون أنت نفسك ...ذاتك ... أي تحصل على **هدفـــــــك .. هدفــــك** الـذي عندما سألتك عنه أجبتني بإجابات بعيده عنك ... هذه الإجابات هي إجابات لسؤال آخر قد يكون (يوماً ما ماذا تتمنى أن تكون ؟!) عندها يمكنك أن تجيبيني (طبيبت .. او وزير ... أو مهندس)

فالهــــدف يتعلق بالحاجـه ... مـاهـــــــو هدفـــــــك الآن ؟! ... أي ماهي حاجتـــك الآن ؟!

كيف ترى نفسك في المستوى التالي لمستواك الحالي ؟!

فيكون مقدار حصولك على هدفــــك بمقدار حاجتك له...وهذا هومعنى الإنجاز بالتحديد ... هدف يعني حاجة

شخص محتاج لأن يعيش في مستوى معين ..... في حاله معينه .. تراه يحرص على أمور معينه دون غيرها ..... لان هدفه معه دائماً.... يصلح البيئه التي من حوله.ويجعلها متلائمه

كمن يريد طلاء غرفته .. فهو يخطط ... يحدد اللون والوقت للبدء ... ثم يبدأ بالطلاء

فهو حصل على هدفه الا وهو طلاء الغرفة

وهذا سيجعله سعيداً

فالانجازات الصغيرة تقود للانجازات الكبيرة والمعتاد على الانجاز .. تراه في تغير مستمر .. حتى انه يغير طريقه لبسه لتناسب هدفه ... الا وهو ان يكون مرتاحاً في هذه الملابس .. او يكون من الطبقة الراقيه .. او يكون بسيطة المظهر .. فهذا يعود لك انت ولهدفك

للمحب يتحـــرر مـن الخجل مـن هذه العلاقه أو يتجاوز عيوب من يحب لأنه بحاجة لهذه العاطفه أو لهذا الحب

هذه كلها حاجات لدى الإنسان تجذبه بشده فهو لاينفك على العمل على تحصيلها بكل حركه وسكنه مـن سكنات حياته . والإنسان القوي الهمـة هو الـذي يربط حاجته الـى إنجازات حقيقيـه في الحيـاة إنجازات دائمـة يستطيع الإستناد عليها لينتقل لإنجاز جديد أكبر .. فلاينساق للعواطف ... ولايضيع في خضم الفوضى من حوله ..

وبالرجوع الى أمثلتنا

الطالـب المجـد يدرس بجد وقد ينجح بتفوق لكن إذا سألته لمـاذا ينجح بتفوق يجيب أن المجتمـع يطلب منه ذلك ... والأولى تحديد مـاهو هـدفك مـن هـذا التفوق .. هـل تريد الحصول على فرصة عمل للحصول على المال .. أم تحب مزاولة مهنة معينة بعد التخرج .

أم أن تفوقك هـو مجرد لإرضاء المجتمع ..فإذا كان ذلك هو هـدفك فأستطيع أن أقول لك أنك بعيد كل البعد عن الإنجاز في حياتك حتى لو كنت الأول على الإطلاق في تفوقك .

والذي يحاول جني المال ليصبح ثرياً فقط ليكون ثرياً ... فتراه يجمع المال بـدون أن ينفقه في ماينفعه .. .وهذا الشخص تراه يـدور في حلقة مفرغة هو لايتقدم في الحياة .. بينما مـن يكرس جهده لجني المال وهو يفكر في تطوير ذاتـه مـن الناحية المادية ليملك الحرية المادية في الإنفاق على نفسه وعلى عائلته فهو سينفع نفسه وينفع الآخرين.. وهذا سيكون اكثر استقراراً .. وأكثر حرية .. سيكون إنسان أقـوى في تحصيل مايريد .. وسيرتقي أكثر في طريق الإنجاز والتقدم في الحياة ... لذلك كان الهدف المادي لـه اهمية خاصة في الحياة ... لأنه نوع من الأهداف التي يتعلق بها تحقيق أهداف أخرى .

ولمـن يحب .. هل حبك هو للمتعـة الحاليـة فقط ... هل هـذا الحـب يسـاعدك على إنشـاء عائلة تستند اليها فـي المستقبل للمضي قـدماً في تحقيـق أهداف وإنجازات جديـدة .. أم أن كـل هدفك هو الحصول على عاطفة مؤقتة تستمتع بها آنياً .. ولاتنظر فيها للمستقبل .

وفـي هـذه الحالـة أنـت تضيـيع وقتك ... لأنـه عنـدما تهدأ هذه العاطفة ويختفي بريقها.. وهـي النهاية الطبيعية لأي علاقـة سوف تكتشف انك أضعت الكثير من حياتك في شئ لم يقدم لك أي شـئ فـي حياتـك . وستكتشف أنك لاتـزال تقبـع في مكانك . ... وهـذا ليـس بالشعور الجيد لمن يريد احراز أكبر عدد من الإنجازات في الحياة .

وربما يقـول قائـل هـي مجـرد علاقـة عاطفيـه مالها والإنجاز ... أقول لك العلاقـة العاطفيـه هـي أيضاً مـن الأهداف الخاصـة التـي يتعلق بها تحقيق أهداف أخرى فهي تعني إستقرارك النفسي ... تعنـي رؤية واضحـة .. تعنـي تحديـد لخطوات حياتـك وماتحتاجـه بالإضافة لهذه العلاقـة .. فترى العلاقـه الناجحة ينتقل صاحبها لتأسيس عائلة .. وبإعتقادي العائلة الصحيحة هي اللبنة الإساسية لتحقيق كـل الإنجازات في الحياة .. فهي تقودك للحصول على ابناء ناجحين .. والى التركيـز في تطويـر حالتـك الماديـة وتطوير عملـك .. وتطوير مستقبلك .. بدلاً مـن أن تكون عالقاً فـي علاقـة إما تستهلك كل تفكيرك وطاقتك وعاطفتك ووقتك بينما أنت تقبع في الحقيقة فـي نفـس المستوى.....أو تجعلك كـل الوقت مشغول بمشاكل لاتتقدم ولا تؤخر .. تفقدك استقرارك النفسـي كـل الوقـت .. لـذلك كانـت العلاقـة العاطفية أو شـريك الحيـاة هـي من الأساسيات التي وجب التركيز عليها كأنجاز حقيقي يسند معظم الإنجازات التاليه في حياتك .

SET YOUR GOAL ... TAKE ACTION...ACHIEVE IT

(SUHAIR ALHASAN)

الهـــدف مُتعـــلِّق بالحـــاجة ...

هدفك الآن .. هو ماهية حاجتك الآن

(سهــير الحـــسن)

هـذه الطريقـه في التفكيـر بالهدف تعطيك الترتيـب اللازم .. وتحـدد لـك الخطـوات بدقـة ... فيكـون سعيك منتظم .. مرتب ..

لأنـك قد تحدد هـدف معيـن .. قـد يبـدو لـك بعيـداً .. أو مستحيلاً فتحبط وتقعـد عن السعـي .. بينما الأصل أنك أذا بدأت السعي ... فتأكد من الوصول .... لإن الوصول متعلق بالبداية .

إبـــدأ   ←━━━━━━━━━━━━━━━   تصـــل

وهكـذا فـإن معرفـة مـاهو إحتياجـك الآن في الوقـت الحـالي يحـدد لـك مـاهي خطوتـك التاليـة ... ماهو الانجاز الذي يجب أن تسعى لتحقيقه .. .

وكمـا هـو واضـح جليـاً .. أنـه لاعلاقـة للوضـع الحـالي بتحقيـق هـدفك ... كيـف تـرى نفسـك في المرحلة التاليه لمرحلتك الحالية هذا هو السؤال ؟

لادخـل للعقبـات ولا العراقيـل التي قـد تتعـرض لـها .. المسـألة مسـألة تحديـد هـدف .. مسـألة إصرار وايمـان بهذا الهدف .. سعي لتحقيق هـذا الهدف .. وأخيـــراً إصرار ومواصلة لتحقيقـه .

انتبـه واقعـك ليـس لـه دخـل ... الموضـوع مـاذا تريـد .. مـاهو احتياجـك ..ومن ثم سعـي مـن بعـد الاستعانة بـالله عـز وجـل .. سعـي دئـوب وحقيقـي (واقعـي) مـرتبط بـالعلم والنزاهـة والوضـوح .. هذه جميعا تجعل هدفك في متناول يديك .

وبمجرد انـك عرّفت هدفك وقررت السعـي باتخـاذك القـرار بـالخطوة الاولـى .. انا ابشرك هنا باذن الله انت تقريباً وصلت .. او في طريق الوصول على اقل تقدير ..

هنا اشير انـه النجـاح قـد يكـون حليفـك بالتأكيـد .. لكـن لسبب مـا يعلمـه الله قـد يتأخر او يتعثـر هـدفك .. هنـا نتشبـث بالمرونـة والرضا والقبـول والسكينـة .. لـذلك دائمـا اقول لاتضـع البيض في سلـة واحـدة ... حافـظ علـى نفسـك .. علـى معنوياتـك ... حالتـك النفسيـة مهمـة ... سعادتك الحاليـة مهمة ...

حتى بعض الاوقـات التي تستخف بهـا مثـل ضحكات الاصدقاء السخيفة هي مهمة .. كـل شـئ يتعلـق بـك مهـم .. فلاتستهين ابـداً .. ودائمـا استمتـع الحيـاة بكـل ماتعطيك .. عائلـة صداقـة ..

اطفـال .. صـحة .. طبيعـة .. رياضـة ... رحـلات ... كـل شـئ جميـل في هـذه الحيـاة .. والعثـرة غذا ستكون خطوة واسعة باذن الله ..

الحيـاة لاتتوقـف علـى شـخص .. ولاتتوقـف علـى منصـب معـين او عمـل معـين أو مشـروع معـين .. الحياة غزيرة ومليئة بالجمال وبالوفرة

كلمـا كـان لاحظـت الـنعم حولـك واسـتمتعت بالتفاصـيل .. زادت مرونتـك وقبولـك .. وحلولـك الثانوية .. ومع الحلول الثانوية تفتح الابواب المغلقة .

وسـترى نفسـك بـين ليلـة وضـحاها تقيـل العثـرة .. وترتفـع درجـة وتقتـرب اكثـر مـن السـعادة التـي تطمح لها .

2-THE GOAL OR NEED...AND HOW MUCH ASSOCIATE TO YOU:-

Needs associate to work... As much you need it... As much you work to get it ....

You may see someone working 10% of his day... And other one works 25% of his day. To get his goal

Achieving that goal will depending on action that you take to move on towards it.

And so on as much as your action .... The amount of your achieve will be

Do you see the person who has this urgent need or the urgent goal in his mind ... working day and night on it?!

(Working here mean planning or thinking about ... It's just filled out his mind)

Like (when you manage your time .. and clean the house .. and organize your stuff ... to make sure that you are free totally afternoon .) so you can feel that happiness and success when you feel like you did everything as supposed to ... and you fixed your environment to belong to feel better ... so step by step .. You can keep going with your goals... To walk forward ... the only thing that you have to notice is how to pick the right goal for right now. So it not luck or just by the way... it is by plan ... and thinking about ...

Its controls the whole course of your life and make it one way or another pour in interest for this goal.

Like I want to set my own room as I want... So I can find a time and effort to fix that room to be mine

Or when I make the first hour in the morning free from anything (it's my time)

Series change in the life begins by these small steps or goals while you don't feel yourself.

So set your goal... (Small goal) (What you need for right now) and take action.

Get your goal!

Like my goal now to paint my room

Take action... Plan. (Pick the color) ...

2-الهــــــــــدف او الحاجـــــــــــــه ... ومدى تعلقـــــك بـــــه

علـــى قـدر حاجتـك لهـذا الشـئ أو هـذا الشـعور أو ذاك ,,,,يكـون مقـدار عمــــلك للحصول عليـــــه

أي كلما زادت حاجتـــــك .... زاد عمـــــلك لأجل الحصول عليه

هكذا أن تعمل بدافع كبير .. .وبنفس الوقت .. أنت تسعى لتحقيق إنجازات في حياتك . ....

قـد تـرى شخص يعمل عُـشر يومـه .. وتـرى الآخر يعمـل لهدفه رُبـع يومـه .. وهكذا على قدر تعلـقك بالهـدف أو حاجتك له يكون مقدار عملك

فتـرى الشخص الذي لديه هذه الحاجه الملحه أو الهدف الملح في عقله ... يعمل ليل نهار ... ؟!

بـل يخطط ليـل نهـار .. لايخطـو خطـوه واحـده إلا وتكـون في خدمـه هـذا الهـدف أو (الحاجـه) فهو يتحكم في كل مجريات حياته ويجعلها بطريقه أو بأُخرى تصب في مصلحه هذا الهدف .

تبدأ سلسله التغيير في حياتـه مـن حيـث لايشـعر .. بملبسـه .. فتـراه يلبس الثيـاب أو الستايل الـذي يقربـه مـن هدفـه ... العلاقـات .. فتـراه يعمل المستحيل ليحصل على هذه العلاقـه أو تلك ..أو قـد تـراه يـدرس بجد (يتـرك اللهـو واللعـب .. يتـرك العمـل .. يتـرك العائلـه والأصدقـاء ..) . هو لايشعر بنفسه

لكنـه بطريقـه أو بـأخرى هـو منجـذب بقـوه الحاجـه التـي في نفسـه .. والتـي يريـد أن يشبعها ..هو يريد أن يكون ذاته ... هنا أصبحت الحاجه هدف ..... هدف لابد من تحقيقه .

هدفـــــــــك ... هـو إحتيـــــاج ... فالهـدف هنـا ضـــرورره لـك ... وليـس مـن الكماليات الثانويه ..

لذلك من يعيش هدفه كل دقيقه ... يحققه ...وهنا يكمــن الجمال

When you want to start?

And start.

Simply … easy

You got your goal!

Another Example:-

The Relationships… You can see someone doing a lot to get this relationship or that. To get love or friendship… Money… Its depend on your goal… so pick the right goal, the goal that can build your life in the future.

So the persons in one way or another strongly attracted to their needs… So you wants to satisfy yourself…… Here your needs become your goal….. A goal that must be achieved for you.

So who lives his goal every minute …he can achieve … And here lies the beauty.

Because it is often the people who have achieved small goals or achievements in their life … ready to achieve new goals… They are ready to achievement….

They know how they feel the victory of achieves that goal even if it was Very simple, such as getting a new jacket or a new job that they worked hard to get it and already they did got it

Then automatically Will moves to the new need or a new goal that would like to get it and starts working for it

We can notice the person who want to be change, the first thing he going to change is his style in clothes… he can wearing clothes or style that brings him closer to his goal.. (Comfortable … or high class … or simple without show off … or just make him happy) its depend on him…

So small goals makes you changes all the time…

You used to achieve so you running forward in changes in life

Change style or places or maybe relationship or work… Or thoughts…

When you change your life style… Its wide step forward… Like when you quit smoking… or follow a diet… Or fast in Ramadan

You can feel yourself new person or new feelings … so you going to own new space in your life or in your feelings you can feel yourself like you are breathing… So it's you will feel that you want new thing new (goal) … And new victory …

لأنه غالباً ماترى الأشخاص الذين حققوا أهداف او إنجازات في حياتهم ...مستعدين لتحقيق أهداف جديده .. فهم مهيأيين لتحقيق الأهداف .... يعرفون مدى لذه تحقيق الهدف .. يشعرون بنشوه الأنتصار .للحصول على هذا الهدف أو ذاك حتى لو كان الهدف شئ بسيط جداً كالحصول على سترة جديده أو عمل جديد هو عَمِل بجد للحصول على ذلك وحصل عليه فعلاً فيكون لديه الإستعداد وتكون لديه حاجه جديده أو هدف جديد يود الحصول عليه ويبدأ عملياً بالحصول عليه .

For me I can classified this person as a successful person... Open mind ... full of life ...

People who used to achieve ... they know what they want exactly for right know...

They can't see the obstacles because their goals are urgent and relate to their desires or needs (relate to their life).

That's why the young people can easily get their goals because there is no responsibility or they are free... Nothing can stop them ... they have the freedom... The time ... and the energy.

When they decide so they going to do... So focus in goals in your life... That can build ... your life ... goals relate to you ... yourself... Your life. ...

Enjoy the life

These are all the needs of the human being that attracts you strongly, so

The real strong person is who determine his real goals ... and work for it

Goals that mean in life... Goals that can build and grow the abundance in life

Like family...

When I start early planning to have my own family... Looking for the right spouse or to get some money that I can start with it .... .

It's like shortcut in the life because this goal can be opportunity to get more and more in life if you plan for it right way!

And if you know how to overcome the obstacles that you can face ... because it's not easy step.. But still important step

For the one who want to get money... Its nice goal because you can help yourself and your family to get better life... So it is kind of goals that can build in life

The one who fall in love ... so he can keep going in the relationship without plan ...

Or he can plan for family

This way of thinking about the target gives you the order. The steps are precisely defined for you because you might set a target. It might seem to you far. Or impossible, so you're frustrated. While the truth is that if you start seeking ... Make sure that you will arrive.... Because access is about the beginning, Start calling.

And you will reach what you call for

SET A GOAL ... THAT YOU
NEED... AND WORK FOR IT

(SUHAIR ALHASAN)

3-THE FLEXIBILITY AND THE OPTIONS THAT AVAILABLE:-

The flexibility here imposes itself on the owner of the goal compulsory and not optional ... because you are already define the goal that you needs. So you will controls all the elements in your life to get this goal so you should be more resilient, has a wide range of options... And unrestricted by one option... That wide range of options give-way to you ... Expansion of your circle... Liberate your goal from all restrictions ... to be achieve

These options are automatically coming to your mind because of the urgent goal that fills out your thinking and your entity (your need), it became as if you had a map in your brain and if you found the road here closed ... you were not despair, but continue ... your effort is to find another way.

Have you heard the saying (I'm not a hero but I have to),

The way to accomplish is a warrior way... He must find a way to breathe (air here means the achievement) and thus multiple options ... In every situation faced by a wide area of choices.,

Because He sought to achieve his goals depending on himself...

These types of individuals are experts by their personal experience... So they...

Believing in themselves on the one hand

And they believe that the experience of each person is different than the others in another hand...They will feel the others.... The need for this individual, or his goal is different from any other one. Therefore, their choices are individually ... **They are the decision-makers to take**

And thus **(flexible options)**...One of the most important features of people who prepared for achievement in life

3ـ كيـف احـدد مـاهي المرحلـة أو المسـتوى التـالي الـذي اود الإنتقال اليه :-

لكي اسـتطيع تحديـد مـاهي الخطـوة التاليـه فـي طريـق تحقيـق أهـدافي لابـد أن أعـرف مـاهو المسـتوى التـالي الـذي أود أن أنتقـل اليـه ... فـي أي فـرع مـن فـروع حيـاتي .. لابـد أن احـدد بالضـبط مـاهو هدفي التـالي .. أو المسـتوى التـالي الـذي أود الإنتقـال اليـه .مـاذا اريد الآن .. ايـن أريـد أن أكـون أو مـاذا أريـد أن اكـون .. اي فـي الصـباح عنـدما تسـتيقظ فكّـر .. كيـف تـرى نفسـك غـداً .. وأتخيـل نفسـي هنـاك فـي هـذه المرحلـة أو فـي هـذا المسـتوى (الـذي أود الإنتقـال اليـه) وأتأمل نفسي من هناك ...

يعني فرضـا لـو انـي حـددت أنـي أريـد أن افتح مشـروع عمـل جديـد نـاجح مثلاً .. هنـا أنـا اتخيـل نفسـي فـي هـذا المشـروع .. واعيش تفاصـيله ثـم انظر لنفسـي الآن مـن هنـاك .. أي كـأني حققـت مـاأريد واتذكر نفسي كيف كنت ..

هـذا التمـرين ... يسـاعدك علـى تحديـد مـاذا يمكنـك أن تفعل الآن بالضـبط ... يـدفعك بقـوة لإن تكـون فـي المرحلـه أو المسـتوى التـالي بسـهولة .. فهـو يحـدد لـك العقبـات التـي أمامـك ويسـاعدك على تجاوزها ... أو كيفية التعامل معها ...ويوضح رؤيتك .

هـذا التمـرين يـوفر عليـك الكثير مـن الوقـت الـذي قـد تكـون فيـه تائـه .. أو قـد تكـون فـي مسـتوى معيـن وتريـد التقـدم ولكنـك لاتعـرف بالضـبط مـاذا يجـب أن تفعل .. او كيـف يمكنك التعامـل مـع حالة معينة تشعر انك عالق فيها ..

(FLEXIBLE OPTIONS).....ONE OF THE MOST IMPORTANT FEATURES OF PEOPLE HWO PREPARED FOR ACHIEVEMENT IN LIFE

(SUHAIR ALHASAN).

أنـا اعتبـر هـذا التمـرين مـن أكثـر التمـارين التـي تزيـد سـرعة التقـدم نحـو ماتريـد .. وكأنـك تحمـل مصباح في يدك يضيئ لك الظلام .

كيف ترى نفسك في المستوى التالي لمستواك الحالي ؟
أنظر لنفسك الآن من المستوى التالي لمستواك الحالي .. ماذا ترى ؟

(سهــــير الحـــسن)

4-ACHIEVEMENT COMING WITH CONFIDENCE IN YOURSELF.

Self-confidence is the basic factor which an individual achieve his goals through it, but if this factor is lost, He will loss his respect for himself... And every goal achieved will be a fake goal ...that could cause confusing himself

As much as you believe in yourself ... depend on yourself to achieve your goal as much that your achievement could be real...

Earn your freedom, each creature has freedom

Be rely on yourself ... and do not make your comfort depend on anyone ...

... Because you are creature has a freedom

Able to adapt in all situations and circumstances.... Do not be a slave humiliating to anything whatever was it importance...

Dearest yourself...

Have a confidence in yourself that you can figure out things ...

4-إبطئ الوقت .. .واستمتع برحلة الوصول

هـذا الموضـوع مـن أدق الأشياء التـي يجـب ملاحظتهـا .. ويعتبر عامـل مهـم فـي اعطـاءك المرونـة اللازمـه .. وفـي جعلك تحـافظ علـى توازنـك .. ويحافـظ علـى إصـرارك وثباتـك فـي التقدم كيف ...

فـي حـال كنـت تعلـم بالضبـط مـاذا تريـد .. والـى أيـن أنـت ذاهـب .. وبالفعل تعـرف مـاذا يجـب عليـك فعلـه .. وأنـت منطلـق فـي السعـي .. وتعمـل بجـد وإخـلاص فـي سبيـل الوصـول الـى إنجـازك الـذي تطمـح اليـه ..يجـب عليـك ملاحظـة أنـه يجـب عليـك إبطـاء الوقت والإستمتـاع برحلـة الوصـول .. استمتـع بمـا حولـك .. أنـدمج بمحيطك .. وسنذكر لاحقـاً كيف يمكننـي أن أنـدمج بمحيطـي وأهميـة هـذا الإندماج فـي دعـم قوة ذاتـي المعنوية ..

إذا كنـت تفعـل مـاعليـك فعلـه بصـدق .. حـاول إبطـاء الوقـت .. بملاحظـة مـاحولـك .. بعيـش لحظتـك .. وإعطـاءهـا حقهـا كـامـلاً .... علـى سبيـل المثـال لـو كنـت تسبـح إستمتـع بالسبـاحة .. ولـو كنـت تقـرأ إستمتـع بـالقراءة .. خـذ فرصـه أو إستراحة .. لاتفكـر فيهـا بـأي شـئ ... لاتفكـر مـاذا ستفعـل أو مـاذا حصـل , أو أنـك فشلـت فـي هـذه الخطـوة لاسمـح الله .. بـل يجـب أن تكـون مـؤمن أنـه لايوجـد فشل وانمـا هـي مسـألة وقـت لا أكـثر ولا أقـل .. إذا كنـت أسعـى معنـى ذلك أنـي سأصـل .. ومـن المؤكـد أن هنـاك بعض العقبـات أو العراقيـل .. لكن هل هنـاك فشـل مع السعـي ؟ ... الإجابة هـي :- لا

لايوجـد فشـل مع السعـي ... فالحيـاة مليئة بالفرص .

وإنما هـي مشيئه الله .. وحكمتـه .. بإختيـار وقت الوصـول .

أمـا اذا نجحـت فعـلاً فـي خطـوة مـا .. إحتفـل بهـا ... استمتـع بنجاحـك بهـا .. إبتهـج مهمـا كـان الإنجـاز صغيـراً .. ومهمـا كانت الخطـوه التـي نجحـت فيهـا تبدو لـك صغيـرة إحتفـل بهـا ..

استمتـع بوقتـك .. كجائـزة أو هديـه على نجاحـك

CONFIDENCE IN YOURSELF ...YOU CAN FIGURE OUT THINGS

(SUHAIR ALHASAN)

ممارسة إبطاء الوقت وأخذ فرصة للتوقف فيها والاستمتاع بالنجاح .. أو بالاستمتاع باللحظة وتقبل ما أنت عليه الآن ... تمرين رائع يرفع مرونتك ... يجعلك ذا مرونة عاليه .. ذا قوة عاليه في السعي لتحقيق الانجاز .

وحتى تفهم أهمية إبطاء الوقت .. سأقول لك لو كنت ممن يسعون بجد لتحقيق هدفك وإنجازك بدون إبطاء للوقت .. بدون أخذ فرصة تقول لنفسك فيها هنيئا لك ما فعلت ... أو بدون أخذ فرصة تقول فيها لنفسك ... كل شئ سيكون على ما يرام بالرغم من فشل هذه المحاولة . أو بالرغم من عدم تحقيق ما أصبو اليه الآن .. ما سيحصل في هذه الحالة أنك ستصاب بالإحباط مع أول مشكلة .. وستصدم بالعقبات بقوة ..و على قدر ما تكون صلابتك وسرعتك وتركيزك في السعي لتحقيق هدفك سيكون قوة إصطدامك .. وهذا الإصطدام سيكون له وقع وتأثير على نفسك .. قد تفقدك الرغبة في المواصلة ..

بينما إبطاء الوقت والاستمتاع برحلتك للوصول سيعزز قابليتك على القبول والتأقلم وإعطاء كل شئ حجمه الطبيعي بدون تضخيم الأمور ...

ومن جهة أخرى يساعدك على الاستمتاع برحلة الوصول هذا الاستمتاع يجعلك تهتم بتفاصيل حياتك .. تلاحظ النعم من حولك ... توسع افقك .. فلا تكون عالقاً بحالة معينة ..

ملاحظة النعم من حولك يجعلك تدرك أن هناك الكثير من الأشياء التي تستحق .. هناك الكثير من الأمور التي تجري تلقائياً فقط بـــــــــتركها ..

بدون أن أجعل تركيزي محصور بها .. لا بل حصر تركيزي فيها يجعلها تقف محلها وقد اعتقد أنه لا مجال على الإطلاق للتقدم والإنجاز . وفي الواقع أن الحياة لا تقف على شئ معين ... أنما هناك غزارة في مجريات الحياة المختلفة ..و لحكمة الهية .. يكون التيسير في بعض الأمور في الوقت الحالي على حساب أمور أخرى وقتها سوف يأتي لتسير لكن في الوقت المناسب .

إفعل ما عليك فعله وأترك الباقي لله ... حافظ على رشاقة مسيرك نحو تحقيق هدفك ... واستمتع برحلة وصولك الى مبتغاك . وهنئ نفسك على هذا الجد والعمل في تحقيق ما تصبو اليه

For example, you see some of people who like to be close to the wealthy ... or the scholars ... or husband or wife or his beloved ....by his money ... or by his position. .... Or his fame.... He can finds himself there... happy in their presence...and the truth is he losing himself
.

He loses his respect for himself in a certain proportion or in a certain way...
.

I have already pointed out that all this is degrees vary from person to person.

Some of them accept to be a slave 100%, and of them accept 50%, each according to his wishes and or according to his faith in himself ... all according to the principles that he holds.

Your faith in yourself makes you free ... This freedom that God has given us...

You do not need anyone ... and you can get what you want.... Just give yourself an area to feel what your real need is ... and listen to the voice of yourself

Believe in yourself that you are able to get what you want on your own way, and without relying on anyone

You are creature has a freedom ... The whole universe is ready for you ... Just ask ... or determine your needs ... like our god created nature and beauty and gave us absolute love ... if you can enjoy it .. Make sure that he going to be here for you... And there is many and many chances in life to get what you want.

The universe is full of abundance and beauty... Which can be enough to your needs as a human ... just realize to the source of this abundance in your life....

And as much as your freedom ... and your dependence on yourself and your faith in them ... you can get real achievements ... achievements that you cannot imagine.

Only by relying on yourself and your belief in your freedom (of constraints and obstacles) in achieving this or that goal.

إذا كنت تعرف الى أين أنت ذاهب .. إذا كنت تفعل

كل مابوسعك بصدق .

. أبطئ الوقت ..

وتمتع برحلة الوصول ....وثق بالتوقيت المناسب

للرب في الوصول الى ماتريد

(سمــير الحســن)

THE UNIVERSE IS FULL OF ABUNDANCE AND BEAUTY

(SUHAIR ALHASAN)

5-BE ONE OF THE PIONEERS OF ACHIEVEMENT... PUT YOUR FINGERPRINT IN LIFE:-

Be with people who are moving in the path of achievement and change in life.... This is not a joke... No words away from the imagination... It is a realistic word... Words of science ... Talk about the experiences of real people who lived in this life.

The beginning is a decision... Or a declaration of freedom of the self.....

First of all you should not be afraid of the difference... And should not be afraid of being lonely and isolation have that freedom.

This decision in itself is an achievement...because it need a courage to take it

Whereas

Some people are enslaved for a certain habit in society or for a certain custom ... He is taken by the group without stopping for a while to ask himself ... Am I satisfied with this? ... Is this something suitable for me?! .. Is this what I am willing to do ..?!

The customs of the community or the family may be many, and many of the things rejected by our pure nature. So if we couldn't correct or reject that habits surrounds you the whole society will keep going on with that wrong way ... and the more people who decide to get rid of these wrong habits ... the more those people can lead the change in society ...

Like smoking ... or healthy food ... or the sports ... or watching the TV all the time ... or wasting time.

What is the most the humanity's need to the pioneers of change...?

The accomplish makes this world more beautiful and make it more pure

Be a pioneer in this life.

The world does not need more followers or more imitators ... You are the origin here ... all you have to do

Be yourself ... depend on yourself..... Honest with yourself ... Do not make your comfort depend on anything except yourself your comfort is not depend on TV show.... Or on icon on your mobile ..., or on talkative friend.

5- المـــــــــــرونه و الخـــيارات المتـاحه :-

المـــــرونه هنا تفرض نفسها علـى صـاحب الهـدف إجبارياً وليس إختيارياً ... لإننـا سبق وعرَّفنـا الهـدف بإنـه حاجــــة . وهـذه الحاجـه تجعل صـاحبها يتحكم في كـل مجريـات حياتـه لصـالح هـذا الهدف لذلك تـرى صـاحب الهـدف مـــرن لديـه متسع من الخيارات .. غير مقيد بخيار واحد .. هذه السعه مـن الخيارات تفسح المجـال أمامـه ... توسع دائرتـه ..تحرر هدفه من قيوده . ..

هـذه الخيارات ليست إعتباطيه ولكنـه وبسبب الهدف الملح الـذي يملأ تفكيره وكيانـه (احتياجه) صـار كأنـه يملك خريطـه في دماغـه توجهه فإذا وجد الطريق هنا مسدود ... لـم ييأس بل اكمل طريقـه بالبحث عـن مخرج آخـر .هل سمعتم بالمقولـه (مُــكره أخـاك لابـطل) هو فـي طريق إنجـازه يكون محاربـاً .. لابد لـه مـن إيجاد مخرج ليتنفس (الهواء هنا هو تحقق أهدافه) وهكـذا تتعـدد خياراتـه .... فهـو في كـل موقـف يواجهه يملك مسـاحه واسعه مـن الخيارت بفعل أنـه سعى للتحصيل أو الإنجـاز في حياتـه معتمداً علـى ذاتـه .. أي بـدون الإعتمـاد علـى أي أحد الا الله عز وجل .

هذه النوعيه من الأفراد تكون لديهم خبره ناتجه من تجربتهم الشخصيه .. لذلك هم..

يؤمنون بأنفسهم من جهة

ويؤمنـون أن تجربـه كـل شخص تختلـف عـن الآخـر ... فإحتياجـه هذا الفرد أو هدفه يختلف عن أي فرد آخر .لذلك تكون خياراتهم منفرده ... هم اصحاب القرار بإتخاذها

وهكـذا تـــكون المـــــــرونه وسعه الخيارات .. مـن أهـم صفات الأشخاص المهيأيين لتحقيق الأهداف والإنجازات في الحياة .

Do not Restrictive yourself in this dress from that designer... Or evaluation yourself according to that plastic surgery.

You don't need a society that gives you your values, according to who your friends ... and you don't need that society which evaluation you depending on the price of your dress that you wear.

You are precious ... and your time that wasted by the talkative friends is precious ... and your health is precious

And all the world with its secrets is yours, if you realize yourself more

And give it more appreciation

Being yourself all the time is like call for purity in this life ... that leads to get freedom... That freedom can give as some space to be ourselves ... to know what we want ... maybe make us stop to take breath and asking yourself (what for?).

To asking yourself... [Am I happy here] .... [Is that what can make me happy]...

ENJOY THE BEUTY OF THE NATUER... THE WEATHER ... THE HEALTH ... IT IS ASECRET OF HAPPINESS AND ACHIEVE ... THAT WHY OUR LORD CREATE THE BUETY IN THE WORLD ITS IS FOR YOU.

المـــرونه وسعة الخيارات من أهم صفات الأشخاص المهيأيين لتحقيق الأهداف والإنجازات في الحياة

سهيـــر الحســـن

ALL THE WORLD WITH ITS SECRETS
IS YOURS IF YOU REALIZE
YOURSELF MORE, AND IF YOU
GIVE IT MORE APPRECIATION

SUHAIR ALHASAN

6- الثــــــــقه بالنفــــــــس وعلاقته بالإنـــــــجاز

الإيمـان بالـذات هـو العامـــــل الأساسـي الـذي مـن خـــلاله يسـتطيع الفـرد أن يحـــقق أهدافـه ... أو أن يشـبع رغباتـه فـإذا فقـد هـذا العامـل .... فقـد إحترامـه لذاتـه .. وكل هدف يحققه سيكون هدف مزيف .... وليس حقيقي لايفتأ أن يكسر الذات ويحطمها

بمــــعنى آخـــــر

بمقدار إعتمـادك علـى ذاتـك فـي تحصيل هدفـك يكـون إنجـازك الحقيقـي ... الـدائم .. الإنجـاز الـذي ترتاح له النفس وتطمئن ...

كُــن حُـــــرا ..... فقد خُلِقْـــت حُـــراً .

لاتعتـــمد إلا علـى نفسِـــك ... ولاتجعلْ راحـــتك مرهونـه بشـــيئ مـا . ترتاح وتهدأ لوجـوده وتتعب وتضنى بغيابه ... لإنك مخلوق حُـر

قـادر علـى التكييـف فـي جميـع الاوضـاع والظـروف ....فلا تكـن عبـداً ذليـلاً لشـيئ مهمـا كانـت أهميته ...

أَعِـــزْ نفسـك .. يُـعِزَّكَ اللـــــه .

فمـثلاً تـرى البـعض ممـن يهـوون مخالطـه الأثريـاء ... أومخالطـه العلمـاء ...أو ذوي المكانـه الإجتماعيـه هـو يحتـرم هـذا الشـخص أو ذاك ..ويتعلق بـه ..إمـا لمـاله ... أو لمنـــصبه ... أو ..... لرفعـه مكانـــته ..... أو لشـهرته....هو يجـد نفسـه هنـاك مـع هـؤلاء .. يرتـاح ويطمئن بحضرتهم ... ويفقد هدوءه واطمئنانه بغيابهم ...

فهذا يفقد احترامه لذاته بنسبه معينه أو بطريقه معينه ... فتراه متعلقاً بهذا الشخص ... وسعادته كإنسان مرهونه بوجود هذا الشخص في حياته ... أو بالقرب منه .

وسبق وأن أشرت أن كل هذا يكون درجات تختلف من شخص لآخر .

You can wondering why I have to be myself. ... When I can simply do what the others doing

And I will tell you that you are right BUT you will never be one from the PIONEERS

It's an honor to be one of them... Putting your fingerprint in the life ... to do that you need to take the first step

Be yourself ..... Manage your time ... set your own goals ... take action... To get this goal or that,

I can tell you that you can find sense for your life if you have a goal like that or if you have that desire.

It doesn't mean that you will lose fun... Or joy .... Or money

You can keep all these pleasers... Plus you have a reason or purpose to everything that you do

Our God created you for reason [(fill the earth with life) enjoy ... build ... family ... love ...job]

Success!

You don't have to change the world by setting a goal!

Just be happy ... get the first step ... small one... And it going to come one by one automatically.

It is a noble reason ... smoothly ... easy

..... For purpose ... so enjoy it ... it's full of joy ...and happiness

So don't miss all that

Start ... be here... Leave your impact in this life

Its call Raise the ceiling of your ambitions

Like if you want to quit cigarette or losing weight ....or learning new language ... you will do it

Easy because you work for something higher than this

So you pushing yourself by having high ambitions.

لأنها نوع من العبوديه لذلك الشخص .. والأفراد بطبيعه الخلق يختلفون بمدى قبولهم للعبوديه .. فمنهم .. من يقبل أن يكون عبداً 100% ومنهم من يقبل 50% كل حسب رغبته وكل حسب إيمانه بذاته ... كل حسب مبادئـــه التي يحملها .

إيمانك بذاتك يجعلك حـــر ... هذه الحُـــــريه التي حبانا بها اللـــــــه ...

أنت غير محتـــاج لأحد ...ولتحصــــل على ماتريد .... فقط أعـــطِ لنفسك مساحه لتشعـــر بماهيـــه حاجتك الحقيقيه ...وإستمع لصوت ذاتك ... وكتمرين ابتعد قليلا عمن تعتقد انك متعلق بهم .. واجه نفسك بمفردك وسترى الفرق .. ربما ستشعر بالانكسار او بالوحده .. او .. او .. او .. وبالضياع اذا كنت فاقدا للهدف الحقيقي .. اما اذا كنت ذا هدف حقيقي .. ربما سيكون الانكسار والوحده هي ماستعاني منه .. لذلك .. نصيحتي هي اعتمد على ذاتك .. تحـــرر ... فالحرية قـــوة .. قوة في معرفة الذات .. ومعرفة الهدف .. ومعرفة ماذا تريد

آمـــــــن بنفسك أنك قادر على الحصــــول على ماتـــريد بنفسـك وبدون الإعتماد على أي كان الا الله عز وجل

أنت خُــلِــقْـتَ حُراً ..... الكون بأجمعه مهياً لك ... فقط إطلُب .. أو حدد ماهية إحتياجاتك

الكون فيه من الوفرة والجمال .. مايكفيك كإنسان ... فقط تعرَّف على مصادر هذه الوفرة في حياتك (تمرين :- يمكنك الانفصال عمن تعتقد انك متعلق بهم لبعض الوقت وواجه نفسك وحيدا واعط لنفسك الفرصة لمعرفة مواطن الوفرة الحقيقية في حياتك)...

وعلى قدر حُـــــريتك ...وإعتمادك على ذاتك وإيمانك بها ... تحـــصــــل على إنجازات حقيقه ... إنجازات لايمكن أن تتخيلها ...

ثـــــــقتك بنفســـــــك تحررك من القيود والعقبات في تحقيق هذا الهدف أو ذاك

الكــون مهيأ لك ..أُطلب ..وحدد ماهية
إحتيـــاجك ..الكـــون فيه من الوفرة
والجمـــال مايكفيك كإنسان

تعرَّف على مصادر الوفرة في حياتك

[سهـــير الحســـن]

أن يكون لك هدف هذا شئ جميل ... وكل شخص في هذه الحياة لديه أهداف .. قد تكون بسيطة جداً مثال للشباب اليافع بالحصول على ملابس معينة أو أشياء مادية معينة أو قد يكون الهدف اكبر قليلاً كالذهاب في نزهة أو رحلة أو زيارة بلد معين ..

أو قد يكون الهدف العيش في بيت ذا مواصفات معينة ... أو الحصول على علاقة معينة .. أو عمل معين .

كل هذه أهداف مشروعة وجميلة .. ومن الرائع ان يبدأ الأنسان العمل على تحقيق أهدافه .. خطوة بخطوة ..

وسيحققها بالإصرار والمثابرة وبالعلم وتحري الخطوات المؤدية لهذا الحلم أو الهدف ...

لكــــــــــــن !

7- أن تكـون مـن رواد الإنجـــــــــــــــاز (ضَـــــعْ بصْمَــــــتك فـي الحيـــــاة) فهذا شئ آخر (Influential)

هذا هو الهدف الأسمى .. الهدف الـذي قـد يحقق لـك جميع ماسبق في طريـق الوصول اليه ... كيف ذلك ؟!

أقول لك

كـن مـع القوافل التـي تسير في طريـق الإنجـاز والتغييـر فـي الحيـاة .... هـذه ليست مزحـه .. ولا هـي كـلام بعيـد مـن الخيـال ..هـو كـلام واقعـي .. كـلام عِـــلُم ... كـلام مـن تجارب أشخاص حقيقين عاشوا في هذه الحيـــاة ... اسع لتحقيق الإنجاز لذاتك أنت .. لحياتك أنت .

البدايـــــــــه هـو قـرار .. هـذا القرار قـد يتطلب منـك تكـريس بعـض الوقـت .. او المـال أو الاهتمـام .. هـو إذن حريـة أو إعـلان عـن حريـه الـذات مـن جميع ماقـد يقيدها لمـاذا اسميها حريـة الـذات لانـك بمجـرد وضع نيـة انـك تريـد أن تكـون شـخص مـؤثر فـي الحيـاة إذن أنت شـخص ذا تـأثير في الحيـاة هـذا يعنـي انـك إنتقلت بمسـتوى تفكيرك الـى مرحلـة أعـلى ...لـذلك أسـميها حريـة الـذات ... لأن الشـخص فـي هـذه المرحلـة يحـاول الإنسـلاخ عـن مايحيطـه ..بإثبات ذاتـه.. هـو لايفكر أنه مختلف ولا أنه يحـاول إثبـات ذاتـه كشـخص مختلف يطلق عليه (show off)...مهمـا كـان إختلافـه شـئ بسـيط ....إنمـا هـو يحـاول أن ينجـز شـئ مـا .. يحـاول الوصول الـى أهدافه . يحاول إثبات ذاته ..

هـذا القرار بحـد ذاتـه هو إنجـاته هو إنجـاز .. وحريـة للـذات .. لأنها محاولة لتحقيق الـذات وإثبات وجودها .

حيث أن

بعـض الأشـخاص تكـون عبوديتهم لعـاده معينـه فـي المجتمـع أو لتقليـيد معـين ... فهـو ينسـاق مـع الجمـع بـدون أن يتوقـف لوهلـه مـع نفسـه ليسـألها ...هـل أنـا راضٍ عـن هـذا ؟! ... هـل هـذا الشـئ مناسب لي ؟!.. هل هذا ماأرتاح لفعله ..؟! هل هذا هو هدفي ..؟!

50

إسعـــع لتحقيق ذاتك انت بتحقيق أهداف مرتبطة بك انت .. إجـــعلها إنجـــاز لحياتك انت اولاً لاتقلد ولاتعيش على إنجازات الاخرين

سهير الحسن

هو يخاف من الإنسلاخ عن المجتمع .. لذلك يفضل أن ينساق مع الجمع ولو كان على حساب راحته ونفسه ... وهذا ما يُدعى متكاسل عن الإنجاز في حياته .. لايريد أن يترك منطقه راحته ...

عادات المجتمع أو العائله قد تكون فيها الكثير والكثير .. من الأشياء التي يرفضها الطبع النقي .. والاصيل .. فإذا تقاعس أصحاب هذا الطبع عن الانسلاخ عن العادة التي قد تكون عادة خاطئة أو تكون عادة تحث على التقاعس وعدم الإنجاز في الحياة ....وهنا التقليد يقود للخسارة ...و هؤلاء الأشخاص رواد للإنجاز و التغيير في المجتمع ... لان المجتمع بدون اشخاص مؤثرين .. او رافضين للأنسياق للجمع في كل شئ سيفقد قيمه وسيتبع العامَّة بحكم التقليد والعادة .. وسيتحول الى مجتمع

المنجزون المؤثرون أو المخططون لخطوات حياتهم يزيدون هذا العالم جمالاً ويجعلونه أكثر نقاءاً

كن من رواد الإنجاز والتأثير في هذه الحياة ... انتق الافضل لحياتك ... اسلوباً وطريقة ومنهجا . .. فكِّر بما تريده انت وليس الاخرون .

العالم ليس بحاجه الى المزيد من المتفيقهين ولا الى المزيد من المقلدين .... أنت الأصل هنا ... كل ماعليـــــك فعله

كـــــن نفسك أنت ... إعتمد على ذاتك ..... آمن بذاتك.. انت بفكرك بإسلوب حياتك بما تختاره بكل تفاصيلك انت **ثمين** (precious) كما انت .. ... لاتجعل راحتك مرهونه ببرنامج تلفزيوني .... أو بأيقونه على هاتفك النقال ..... أو بصديق ثرثار ...

لاتحصري أهميتك في هذا الفستان من المصمم الفلاني .. او عمليه التجميل تلك التي سوف تجعل لي مكانه في أعين الآخرين .. أو في المجتمع

لاحاجة لك بالمجتمع الذي يعطيك قيمه تبعاً لكونك صديق الفلان المشهور ...ولاحاجه لكِ بالمجتمع الذي يعطيكي قيمه تبعاً لثمن الفستان الذي تلبسيه .. او تبعاً لعمليه التجميل التي تدفعك أحياناً لتعريض حياتك للخطر في سبيل ارضاء هذا المجتمع السقيم .

أنت ثمين ... ووقتك الذي يهدره الصديق الثرثار ثمين ...وصحتك ثمينه

والعالم بآسره ملكك لو تعرفت على نفسك أكثر وأعطيتها تقديرها أكثر .

كل العالم بأسراره هو ملكك ..إذا تـعـرفت على نفسـك أكـــثر و

أعطيتها

تقدير أكـــبر

(سهير الحسـن)

SECTION 2
PURSUEING THE GOALS

الفصل الثاني
قوة تحقيق الأهداف

1-HOW TO SET INTENTIONS THAT SERVING MY GOALS.

Life is like puzzle`s pieces there is a specific intention for every action you play and whenever you put the appropriate pieces in the right place, the game is finished correctly, the more you put the appropriate intention for each deed you do, the faster you will progress in the game of life and you get what you want easily and smoothly, overcoming all obstacles as much as possible.

In this way, you can be sure that you are on the right path towards the achievement in your life

If you intend to set a specific intention for every action you want to do, that's means that you far away from the randomness ...far away from randomness means you know where you are going or in other words you know what you want or what your goal is.

If you put Intention for every action, you serve your goal on a way or another.

Keep yourself away of randomness is one of the reasons for success and achievement

And that without a vision or a major goal will remain you at the same level ... which will keep yourself at a certain level without greater achievement.

In other words

If you aspire to happiness.... Whether this happiness is desired in the house.... which was aspiring to it

And already got it... By your hard work to achieve it.... If you do not have the vision or desire to raise the ceiling of your ambition to something higher will remain at the same level that you got.

Glory be to God ... the nature of humanity always has an ambition.... Whether he wanted it or not.... So often we see for example the house wife that cares about the house ... cannot stop... But continue to amend and improvement... but May moves to another larger and wider

The company owner...Who succeed in his company, but aspires to develop and expand

Who finds his desire to study and science we can see him moves nonstop in search... continues to develop himself.... And nonstop at the limit.

5-كيف أُعد نوايا تخدم هدفي؟!

الحياة مثل قطع لعبه اللغز (البازل) هناك نيه محدده لكل عمل تقوم به وكلما وضعت القطع المناسبه في المكان المناسب

انهيت اللعبه بشكل صحيح

اي كلما وضعت النيه المناسبه لكل عمل تقوم به سوف تتقدم اسرع في لعبه الحياة وتحصل على ماتريد بسهوله وسلاسه متجاوزا كل العقبات قدر المستطاع

وبهذه الطريقة، يمكنك أن تكون متأكدا من أنك على الطريق الصحيح نحو الإنجاز في حياتك

فلتجعل هدفك هو **الإنجاز** ..الصلاة إنجاز ... إصلاح البيت إنجاز .... الحصول على عمل مناسب إنجاز ..الحصول على زواج ناجح ومستقر إنجاز .. ترك التدخين انجاز ... المحافظة على وزنك الصحي ورشاقتك ولياقتك انجاز .. المحافظه على استقرار حالتك النفسيه على مستوى معين من الراحه والبهجه إنجاز وهكذا ...هذه خطوات صغيرة تقودك الى الهدف الاكبر في حياتك

لإنك اذا كنت تنوي نيه محدده لكل عمل تريد ان تقوم به هذا يعني انك بعيد عن العشوائيه   بعيد عن العشوائيه يعني انك تعرف الى اين انت ذاهب او بمعنى آخر انت تعرف ماذا تريد او ماهو هدفك فانت بوضعك نيه لكل عمل تقوم به يعني انك تخدم هدفك بشكل أو بآخر

. البعد عن العشوائيه هو سبب من اسباب النجاح والانجاز. ....

لكن هذا التنظيم بدون رؤيه أو هدف رئيسي سوف تبقيك في نفس المرحله ... اي ستحافظ على نفسك بمستوى معين دون إنجاز أكبر .

بعبارة أخرى :-

لو كنت تطمح الى السعاده .... سواء كانت هذه السعاده المنشوده في البيت أو كحاله إجتماعيه ... أو ماديه ... اي كان ماتطمح له

وحصلت عليه .. بفعل عملك الدئوب لتحصيله .... لو لم تكن لديك رؤيه أو الرغبه في رفع سقف طموحك الى شئ أعلى سوف تبقى في نفس هذا المستوى الذي حصلت عليه

وسبحان الله ... طبيعه الانسان بالفطره ... دائماً له طموح .... سواء اراد ذلك أم لا ....لذلك غالباً مانرى مثلا ربه المنزل التي تهتم بالبيت ... لاتقف عند حد معين .. بل تستمر في التعديل والاصلاح ... لابل تنتقل الى آخر اكبر واوسع

صاحب الشركه ... لايكتفي بنجاح شركته .. بل يطمح لتطويرها وتوسيعها

الذي يجد رغبته في الدراسه والعلم تراه لايقف عند حد ... يستمر في تطوير ذاته .... ولايقف عند حد

فإذا أردت أن تكون لك بصمه في هذه الدنيا ... وتلحق بركب المغييرين .. الذين أثروا في هذه الحياة ... ماعليك سوى

إضمار نيه محدده .... وضع هدف كبير تريد أن تحققه .... في هذه النقطه أنت لاتعرف كيف ستصل إليه .. ولا تعرف الطريق .. حتى أنك لاتعرف البدايه .... لابل قد تكون لاتعرف ماهو هذا الهدف ....

أنا أقول لك حدث نفسك وقل ... أريد ان تكون لي بصمه في هذه الحياة ....لا أريد أن أترك هذه الدنيا بدون أن اكون قد حققت شيئاً أعتز به.. اعتز بتحقيقه

أنا اقول لك ضعها ..... أضمر هذه النيه ... ذكّر نفسك بهذا الهدف .... تأمل فيه .... عشه في مخيلتك . هذا ليس ضرب من الجنون

If you want to have imprint in this world ... and join the pioneers of change in the world, who have enriched in this world ... all what you have to do is...

Intent specific intention + put major goal.

{SUHEIR AL HASAN}

الكون بفعل الخالق ... مسخر لك .... كلما كانت نيتك صادقه .. ونقيه .. ستفتح لك أبواب أنت لاتتوقعها .... تساعدك على تحقيق نيتك

هذه الأبواب موجوده ... معده لك أنت كإنسان .... ولكنها فُــتحت ... بمفتاح نيتك ... المفتاح الذي تملكه وانت لاتعرف .

وأنا اقول لك هنا إستخدم هذا المفتاح ... الذي يعد من أقوى المفاتيح على الإطلاق ... تفتح به مالاتستطيع فتحه فإذا ملكت

المفتاح (النيه) ...

والإراده (تدفعها الحاجه) .... فكلما كانت حاجتك اقوى .. كانت ارادتك لتحقيق ماتصبو اليه اقوى

والمواصله هذا العنصر الذي يفتقر اليه الكثير منا ...كل ماعليك فعله هو (لاتيأس) .. استمر في تصور هدفك .. تخيله ... عيشه ...

مهما كان بعيد المنال بالنسبه لك في الوقت الراهن

هذا الإصرار على طلبه ... يحققه لك ... يجذبه باتجاهك ... وقد يكون من الصعب فهم هذا الكلام او قد يفهم بطريقة خاطئة سأعطيك مثالا بسيطأ ولكنه غاية في الاهمية

لو مثلا قلت انا سأكون انا من المغيرين .. وسوف لن استمع للأغاني لانها مضيعة للوقت ومهدرة للعواطف والفكر .. ولن اشاهد التلفزيون

ربما ستقول لي ان هذا تغير ببدو بسيطا او تافهاً .. لكنه في الحقيقة انجاز و تغير انت لاتعرف قيمته وعندما تبدأ بالتطبيق والسعي لتغيير نفسك نحو هذا الهدف ستكتشف كم من الوقت انت تهدر يومياً في مشاهدة وسماع هذه الاشياء .. وكم من المتعة والانجاز والحياة فقدت بانغماسك بأسلوب حياة هو بعيد كل البعد عن التفكير الصحي .. والحياة الجميلة .. وحتى عن اسلوب الحياة الصحي

لذلك يجب فهم التغيير هنا بمعناه البسيط وتأثيره العميق على الشخص وعلى المجتمع .. يعني تخيل كم تملك من الوقت عن توقفك عن مشاهدة التلفاز تماماً .. وكم من صفاء الذهن سوف تحصل عليه ببعدك عن مايشغله ولا ينفعه ..

انه وقت طويل .. وهكذا .. الحياة البسيطة مثل البيت الجديد الفارغ .. عندما تضع فيه اثاثا جميلا وقطع منتقاة .. والحياة العشوائية مثل جلوسك في مخزن ملئ بالاغراض الى لاتمت بصلة اليك غير انها تشغلك طوال الوقت وتزيد من ضيقك.

I'm sure at this point you will say

I do not know the way... I do not know the beginning.... even you may not know what that goal is!

I would like to tell you that (remind yourself) say: - I want to put my imprint in this life.... I do not want to leave this world without achievement something I cherish it.

Like having great family... Just like my grandfather...

Or success job ... like my dad business.

So this is the major goal

Now you have to start with the small one

Like mange your time .... Or get a step forward ... like job... Maybe you have to quit something or relationship

Get the first step

I would like to tell you to put your imprint...... Add that intention to your mind ... Remind yourself that my god will help me to put that imprint ...Meditation in it ... Allow to your dream to lives in your imagination ..

It's not crazy.

The universe created by our lord the Creator ...He put all that universe in your serve.... to be happy, whenever your intention is honest... And pure... You will open the doors that you do not expect.... which help you to achieve your intention

These doors are exist ... prepared for you as a human.... and it will be opened by the key that you had (your intention) ... The key that you have while you do not know.

I tell you here use that key (the Intention) ... which is one of the most powerful keys at all ...you can Open any door (goal) by it. Easy and smoothly

If you have the key...

And the willing ... (motivate by the need).... And the more your need is urgent... Your desire to achieve will be stronger.

THE UNIVERSE CREATED BY OUR LORD THE CREATOR... HE PUT ALL THE UNIVERSE IN YOUR SERVE

SUHAIR ALHASAN

2-CONTINUITY

(Continuity) that element, which many of us lacks for it ... All what you have to do is (do not despair)... Continue to imagine your goal...

Imagine .and. Live...

No matter how much that your goal seems impossible to be achieve at this moment

This insistence on its request ... brings it to you ... attracts it towards you.

If you have a certain dream or ambition ... and if it did not happen for any reason ... Do not stop ... Do not despair ... Complete your way flexibly ... Acceptance, many options there for you,

That acceptance is like if you used all the potential to serve your goal

Once you despair and turn a blind eye to this goal ... (I cannot get it) that means you lost the key... And you will stay at the level that you are in.

This varies from person to person ... some of them stops on a particular social situation

Like there is no job ... he just watching TV all the time

Or stops at a particular physical state

Like he sick...

Or he don't have language.

(Continuity) may be one of the most difficult elements that must be ... For example, who wants to lose weight ... The diet works for a certain period... And then... Halts in the middle of the road

Stopping here may lead to regression ... gradually returning to his weight... And returning to the same suffering

Who smoke as well?

6- التقبّل أو المرونة : -

لو كان لديك حلم معين أو طموح معين ... ولم يتحقق لأي سبب ... لاتتوقف ... لاتيأس ... أكمل طريقك بمرونه ... بتقبل هذا التقبل هو كأنك تستخدم كل مافي حوزتك لتحقيق هدفك

قَـــبول ماتحصل عليه ... مع عدم اليأس لتحقيق هدفك .....كأنك تستخدم وتسخر كل مايأتيك لتحقيق هدفك ... بل أنت تسير قدماً لتحقيقه

وبمجرد اليأس وغض النظر عن هذا الهدف ...(أنا لا أستطيع الحصول عليه) هذا يعني أنك فقدت المفتاح .. وستمكث في المستوى الذي أنت فيه

أي ستتوقف عن المسير .

وهذا يختلف من شخص لآخر ... فمنهم من يتوقف عند حاله اجتماعيه معينه

أو يتوقف عند حاله ماديه معينه

المواصله قد تكون من اصعب العناصر التي لابد منها ... فمثلا من يريد انقاص وزنه ... يعمل الريجيم لمده معينه .. ومن ثم .. يتوقف في منتصف الطريق

التوقف هنا قد يؤدي الى التراجع ... فيعود تدريجياً لوزنه الزائد .. ويعود لنفس المعاناة

الذي يشرب السكائر أو الشيشه كذلك

تراه يتوقف لفترة معينه ... فإذا كانت إرادته ضعيفه سيعود اليها .

لاتتوقف في تحصيل هدفك . ... والهدف الكبير ... يساعدك بل يدفعك لتحقيق الأهداف الصغيرة .. والأهداف الصغيرة تساعدك على المسير قدماً لتحقيق هدفك الكبير .. فهي سلسله مرتبطه ببعض

هدف كبير .... وأهداف صغيرة تمثل خطواتك لتحقيق الأول . ... فإذا توقفت عند الأهداف الصغيرة ضاع الهدف الكبير .... وربما تفقد اهدافك الصغيرة الواحد تلو الآخر .

لاتتـــــوقـــف

دائما .. عندما ترى نفسك قد اطمئننت وحققت شئياً ما .... لاتركد .. بل فكر بشئ جديد تعمل له .. أضمر نيه جديده .. أو فكره جديده .

وهذا سر جمال الطبيعه الإنسانيه التي حبانا بها الله .

So you do not stumble... But think how you can continue..... Or think about new idea that can help you to continue in your way

This is the secret of the beauty of the human nature which God has given us.

Insisting on continue

هي متسلسلة .. الهدف الكبير يساعدك على المواصلة ... والأهداف الصغيرة توصلك الأول وهكذا

سهير الحسن

3-HOW CAN I BE FASTER IN PURSUIT OF MY GOAL WITHOUT BEING LOST:-

If you want to be faster in pursuit of your goal without being lost

You should know that: -

Any action without a specific intention is wasting time and effort and keeps you away from achieving in your life

Or can make you be lost amid the chaos and mob in the community

Like if you want to quit watching TV

If you just sitting in this night and another night with your family you will never quit

Visiting a friend for long time who watching TV all the time can make you just give up and watching the TV.

So you have to plan your day

This includes every single action in your life.... (The more organized, or more action associated with specific intentions will be more increase in your achievements in life)

For example:-

If you want to eat ... you can set intention that eating healthy food is for getting a healthy body, which makes me person enjoying by his health and his life, and so I got reason of a happiness... Being happy person means a strong person and a reasonable mind can distinguishing things.. And taking the right decisions to get what I want smoothly and easily

And you can set different intention such as I want to be more agility or more beauty.

That's doesn't mean that you didn't set specific intention to your action...

Associate the intention with any deed is very necessary whatever was that intention or deed simple

This may seem a bit weird or difficult to some people but you will automatically do it if you got used to it

If you want to do your workout

3-- كيف يمكنني أن أكون أسرع في السعي لتحقيق هدفي الكبير دون أن أضيع في خضم الفوضى؟

إذا كنت تريد انت تكون أسرع في السعي لتحقيق هدفك بدون أن تضيع في خضم الفوضى يجب أن تعلم أنه :-

اي عمل بدون نيه محدده هو إضاعه للوقت والجهد ويبقيك بعيداً عن تحقيق الإنجاز في حياتك

او يمكن ان يجعلك تضيع وسط الفوضى والغوغاء في المجتمع

وهذا يشمل كل عمل في حياتك .... (كلما زاد التنظيم أوكلما زادت الأعمال المقرونه بالنوايا المحدده زادت إنجازاتك في الحياة)

مثال على ذلك :-

إذا كنت تريد أن تأكل ... يمكنك وضع نية أن تناول الطعام الصحي هو للحصول على الجسم الصحي، مما يجعلني شخص يتمتع بصحته وحياته، وهكذا حصلت على سبب من أسباب السعادة ... شخص سعيد يعني شخص قوي وعقل راجح في تمييز الأشياء .. واتخاذ القرارات الصحيحة للحصول على ما أريد بسلاسة وسهولة

ويمكنك تعيين نية مختلفة مثل أريد أن أكون أكثر خفة في الحركة أو أكثر جمالاً.

وهذا لا يعني أنك لم تحدد نية محددة لعملك ... ربط النية مع أي فعل ضروري جدا مهما كان ذلك القصد أو الفعل بسيط

وهذا قد يبدو غريباً نوعاً ما أو صعباً للبعض ولكنك سوف تفعله آوتوماتيكياً إذا ما إعتدت على ذلك

اذا كنت تريد ان تعمل تمارين رياضيه   نيتك ممكن ان تكون (انا سأقوم بهذه التمارين الرياضيه لأحصل على جسم صحي لاكون اكثر جاذبيه   أو لأشغل نفسي هنا في المكان الذي اريد ان أكون فيه) ... لاساعد على تنظيم طاقتي .. صرف الطاقة الزائدة او السلبية .. واستبدالها بطاقة متوازنة .. صحية ... اجدد نشاطي .. انقي فكري ... ارفع ثقتي بنفسي .. اقرن عدة نوايا في عمل واحد وهذا شئ مستحب .. ووارد

فهو نوع من دفع الذات او النفس بإتجاه الهدف مهما كان ذلك الهدف.

Your intention could be

I'll do it to get healthy body

To be more attractive

To keep me busy here. Where I want to be .it's kind of pulling yourself... Or pushing yourself forward your goal whatever it was.

Linking Intention   Linking intention with every step of my life is very important... No matter how simple this step it was

Suhair alhasan

ربط كل عمل مهما كان بسيطاً بنية محددة هو نوع من دفع الذات أو الإسراع في تحقيق الأهداف بعيداً عن العشوائية أنت تستغل كل دقيقه من حياتك

(سهـــــير الحســـن)

Also!

You can set several small goals that easy to get... And those small goals can leads you to the major goal

Like

I want to lose 1 kilo in the week

The major goal is losing 12 kilo

Workout for 20 minutes at the morning and 20 minutes afternoon

The major goal is working out for an hour daily

Serial small goals leads to the big goal... The big goal helps you to continue in the small goals

Suhair AL Hasan

4-HOW CAN I GET MY GOAL SMOOTHLY ... WITHOUT OBSTACLES.-

Going beyond what coming to you naturally can smashed everything beautiful in your life and make it hard for you

So if you want a life without hurting as much as you can

And if you want your life going on forwards smoothly and easy don't go beyond what coming to you naturally

Maybe it (the thing that you want to get) will not be perfect as you want but at least it will be normally... Easy ... smoothly

Without hardship

FOR EXAMPLE:-

Like someone want to fall in real love and then he can decide the marriage

And he already have a chance with someone who is good and suitable to him ...

Stopping his life to get something maybe he can't find it.

Nice person and someone who can be beside you all the time, care about you, spending the rest of his life with you more worthy

Maybe it's not perfect but at least are not stuck in the same point in life

Its hardship especially when everybody get his place in life except you.

We have to know that the wonderful things are not perfect...

Be real

Get what coming to you normally without complication

Be here!

The life is simple ... and wonderful .... You don't need a lot to be happy.

4- كيف احصل على ه   ـدفي بسهوله وبـــدون عقـــــبات ؟!

الذهاب الى وراء ماياتي اليك تلقائياً أو بشكل طبيعي يمحي ويقضي على كل شئ جميل في حياتك ويجعل الحياة صعبه عليك ولذلك في حياتك اذا اردت ان تسير الى الأمام بسهوله وبسلاسه وبدون عقبات لاتذهب الى وراء ماياتي اليك بشكل طبيعي ابداً , ربما ماتحصل عليه لن يكون كاملاً بالشكل الذي كنت تتوقع   او قد يأخذ وقتاً اطول مما كنت تتوقع ... لكن على الاقل سيكون بشكل طبيعي وتلقائي وسهل   بدون صعوبات... خذ ماياتيك بشكل تلقاءي .. لاتضيع الفرص .. وبنفس الوقت توقع ماسيأتيك ... مثلاً انه سيكون اقل نوعاً ما من توقعاتي او ليس بالمستوى الذي اطمح .. ومن جهة اخرى توقع العكس انه سيأتي اعلى واكبر من توقعاتك ... وفي كلا الحالتين توقع ردة فعلك

.. فإذا كان يناسبك .. امضي قدماً .. واحصل على ماتقدمه الحياة لك سواء كان اقل او اكثر من توقعاتك مادام يصب في مصلحتك .. لكن اذا كان يعيقك او يعرقل مسيرك فانت متنبئ مسبقاً .. لذلك سيكون من السهل تلافي الاخطاء او على اقل تقدير ستجتاز الموقف باقل الخسائر.. فالاصل ان تغتنم كل ماياتيك ... .مهما كان .. مادام يحقق لك نسبه من الانجاز في حياتك سواء كان هذا الانجاز معنوي او مادي.

مثال على ذلك

دعنا نتكلم عن العلاقه بين الرجل والمرأة وفقاً لما يأتي اليك بشكل طبيعي هناك حدود للعلاقة بين الرجل والمرأة وهذه الحدود ,.هي ليست قيود بقدر ماهي حدود وجدت للحفاظ على بعضها البعض آمنة دون الشعور بالضرر لكلا الجانبين الرجل والمرأة

لأننا كبشر ضعفاء من ناحيه المشاعر ..... والغريزة من ناحية أخرى.

في حالة الخلط بين الرجال والنساء لأي سبب من الأسباب (العمل أوالدراسة أوالصداقة) وفي حالة عدم احترام طبيعة كل جانب من شأنه أن يؤدي إلى إلحاق الضرر بمشاعر أحد الطرفين أو كلا الطرفين قد يستمر هذا الضرر تأثيره على الحياة بأكملها

وبعبارة أخرى تغيّر جذريا الشخص من شخص إلى آخر مختلف تماما بحيث يمكن أن يفقد الفرد نقائه اوبالتالي!

ولتجنب كل هذا علينا أن نعطي أنفسنا أو مشاعرنا أهمية وإعتبار .... كل شيء قادم بشكل طبيعي يمكن أن يكون ... جميلا ... سهل ... لذلك علينا أن نتوقع ما يمكننا الحصول عليه .... ووضع خطة للتعامل مع ذلك

82

For another example:-

Like in my studying I expect what will coming to me naturally. I have to expect (the success) and (fail)

… If I studied hard I will succeed.

The Careless, leads to fail……

You will be more flexible and more acceptable

And you are faster now in Pursuit accomplishment … Because you have a vision. You expected what came to you naturally and accept it early.

ارجع إلى مثالنا   عن العلاقه بين الرجل والمرآه   إنها مجرد نوع من النعمة لأننا يمكن أن نتوقع ما سوف يحصل من طبيعتنا ..... غالبا ما تنمو هذه العلاقه لتكون صداقه

علينا أن نتوقع ذلك ... وعلينا أن نكون حذرين جداً

انها عن أنفسنا... عن مشاعرنا

ما زلنا نتحدث عن (العقبات)وكيفيه تجاوزها من خلال هذا المثال البسيط ، وأن هناك نية وراء كل فعل علينا أن نحترم ونقدر... خاصة إذا كان كل جانب يعرف أن العلاقة مستمرة .. وكلنا نعرف أن الصداقة يمكن أن تتحول بسهولة إلى (الحب) إذن نحن من البداية لدينا فكرة حول ما سيحدث.

لذلك الأمر متروك لكل شخص..... إذا كان يريد أن يتجاوز ما يأتي إلى نفسه بشكل طبيعي مثل أنه لا يتوقع أي شيء من نفسه وليس لديه أي رؤية حول مستقبل تلك العلاقة .... بالتأكيد يمكن أن يؤدي إلى الخلط بين المشاعروسوف يستمر بهذه العلاقه دون مراعاة لمشاعر نفسه ودون مراعاة لمشاعر غيره ... ودون تخطـــيط .. وهذا بالتالي سيقود الى شئ أول مايوصف بأنه (لم يكن بالحسبان) مع أن الحقيقه انه كان بالحسبان .. وكان لديك عده مؤشرات تدق لك أجراس الإنذار في كل مرة من طبيعتك .. من غريزتك .. وأنت تجاهلتها .... فلاتلوم في هذه

الحاله إلا نفسك ..... فإما أن يؤدي الى إرتباط لم يخطط له على الصعيد العملي ... أو الى فرقه مع أذيه للمشاعر لأحد الطرفين أو كلاهما ... وفي كلا الحالتين هناك خسارة عاطفيه قد تكون كبيرة في بعض الأحيان ... كان بالإمكان تجاوزها بقليل من الإصغاء لمشاعرنا .

نحن نحدد نوعين من العلاقات..... (وفقا لما يأتي لك بشكل طبيعي)

و(وفقا لما مايأتي بتجاوز ما يأتي لك بشكل طبيعي

والثاني هو حول .... أنا لا أتوقع أي شيء من هذه العلاقة أو من نفسك ولكن سوف تستمر في ذلك

وبهذه الطريقة تجعل نفسك كروبوت آلي   الذي لا يمكن أن يشعر

أنت تتجاهل طبيعتك كإنسان..هذه الطبيعه التي لابد من الإصغاء لها ووضعها ضمن إطار صحيح .. لاتتجاهلها تحت أي مسمى ً كان ..... ولاتتركها عشوائيه بدون تنظيم ..لأن تنظيم هذه المشاعر وجد بالفطرة فقط للأنسان تمييزاً له عن بقيه المخلوقات

لأنك عن طريق تجاهل مشاعرك سوف تصل إلى تلك النقطة التي لا يمكن أن تستمر فيها   لذلك في عدم وجود نية في العلاقة من هذا القبيل يمكن أن يربك مشاعرك .. وبالتالي يربكك ويحول تركيزك عن السعي لنيل ماتطمح اليه ..

. وفقط من خلال تجاوز ما يأتي لك بشكل طبيعي أنت تضع العقبات في طريقك بينما انت لا تشعر

84

GET WHAT COMING TO
YOU NATURALLY.

(SUHAIR ALHASAN)

وبعض الناس يمكن أن تعطي الكثير من الأعذار فقط للحفاظ على تلك العلاقة أو للحفاظ على هذا الشخص في حياته بغض النظر عن أي نوع من تلك العلاقة (الحب أو الصداقة فقط أو شخص أنا أعرفه عن طريق الصدفة)

وربما يستطيع أن يتجاهل نفسه لكنه لا يستطيع تجاهل الناس من حوله

إذا كنت تريد أن تكون كما الروبوت يمكنك ذلك

ولكن لا يمكنك جعل الناس من حولك كما الروبوت أيضاً.

... وسوف يكون من الصعب جدا بالنسبة لك وبالنسبة لهم ....انت وضعت عقبة في طريقك وفي طريق الاخرين

لاتذهب الى وراء مايأتي اليك تلقائياً او بشكل طبيعي. وهذا سيسبب الصدمة أو الانكسار .. او الحزن .. وبقاءك مريضاً مهزوزاً .. ربما غير مبال .. لا يجدي نفعاً وان تظاهرت بالقوة والسعي لتحقيق ماتريد ..لذلك اقول لك وجب تحررك .. تحرير نفسك من هذا العبء الثقيل .. هذا الهم الذي يلهيك عن التقدم والتحصيل في حياتك .. .. ربما تحصل على علاقة اقل عاطفية من الاولى .. واقل تعلق .. لكن فيها من الاستقرار و والتقدم والتحصيل المادي والمعنوي في حياتك وحياة عائلتك .. .... هذا المثال واضح بالنسبة للجميع في المجتمع وتأثيره يمتد الى جميع افراد الاسرة .. ويرفع سقف الاهداف التي تحقق .. يعني شئ يتعلق به عدة اهداف .. الا وهو حريتك الذاتية وتأثير ذلك في تحصيل الاهداف

توقع كل شيء من نفسك (لاتهملها) .وتعامل مع هذا التوقع .. إجعل مساحة في حياتك .... لا تضع العوائق في طريقك ...لابد من الحفاظ على نية محددة وراء كل فعل

.

مثال رقم (2):- في دراستي أتوقع ما سيأتي لي بطبيعة الحال .. لا بد لي من توقع النجاح والفشل

الدراسه بجد تؤدي الى النجاح.

.......(اللا مبالاة)، يؤدي إلى الفشل .

انت الان اكثر مرونه واكثر قبولاً ...انت الان اسرع في السعي للإنجاز في حياتك لانك لديك رؤيه ... انت توقعت ماسيأتي اليك بطبيعه الحال ... وتقبلته مسبقاً .

ENGAGEMENT THE INTENTIONS WITH EACH DEED

NEVER GO BEYOND WHAT COMING TO YOU NATURALLY

JUST EXPECT EVERYTHING FROM YOURSELF (DON'T NEGLECT IT) AND DEAL WITH THAT EXPECTATION

EARN A WIDE SPACE IN YOUR LIFE

YOU HAVE UNLIMITED OPTIONS ...MOVE IN THAT WIDE SPACE ...

DON'T PUT OBSTACLES IN YOUR WAY

MAINTAIN SPECIFIC INTENT BEHIND EVERY ACTION GIVING YOU SPACE AND ABILITY TO REMOVE THE OBSTACLES FROM YOUR WAY EARLY

SECTION 3
THE POWER OF PURSUING GOALS

الفصـــــــل الثالث
قـــوة تحـــقيق الأهـــداف

1-THE ACCEPTANCE AND OVERCOMING OBSTACLES AND DIFFICULTIES:-

Acceptance is one of the most helpful things to overcome obstacles and difficulties

It's kind of high consciousness dealing with realty in which you are living whatever it was that reality,

It's hard.

Accepting a situation you are not satisfied about it ... or accepting a job you do not find yourself in it ... while you have to stay in it ... Here you have nothing but acceptance as a solution for that confusing situation.... Because all the time in our life we have a lot of problems or obstacles stops us.

Stops our ambitions.

So to keep going ahead in our life we need a lot of acceptance to live according to our principles...

In fact you have to have enough strength

Acceptance in this situation does not mean surrender ... because in fact you accepted... And dealt with that situation calmly ... even you brought the joy and love as much as possible to what you temporarily accepted ... and try to reform it as much as you can

And at the same time you are looking for the best with all your potential ... So you are looking here and there... Not to find the alternative.... but to find the best, used what you accepted as a joy, you enjoyed it (and already kept it)

An example of this is: - Who works in his job does not find himself in it... Some advices says that you have to leave what you can't find yourself in it directly and looking for what satisfies your ambition...

But I have a different opinion. (This opinion came from my personal experience). I prefer to stay in what I am currently doing ... trying to accept ... and trying to bring the joy to what I do ... so that you can continue it and you can give it as it should But at the same time .. I continue hardly looking for what change this situation... Do not despair ... and do not give up to moving to the next level ... Reminding yourself gently... Compassion... Flexible. That (This situation does not suit me...).

1- - (القبـــــــول) والتغــــلب على العقـــــبات والصعوبات:-

أنا لا أحبذ ... أن تترك فوراً مايزعجك .... أعطِ نفسك فرصه أن تجد الأفضل أولاً .... إستغل الفرص السانحه (عصفور في اليد خيرُ من عشرة على الشجرة) .... وان كانت الاشجار كُـــــثر .. وإن كنت صياداً ماهر لاتقحم نفسك في صعوبات أنت في غنى ً عنها ..... إحتفظ بكل مايأتيك من الحياة . وواصل البحث عن الأفضل .

مواصله البحث عن الأفضل يعطيك مدى واسع من الخيارات ... بالإضافه لما تملكه بالفعل ... ولما جاء اليك بطريقه طبيعيه وبطريقه تلقاءيه .

إقبـــــل ...... تقبـــــّل .... وإبحث عن الأفضل ... فالحياة مليئه بالخيارت الواسعه ... والحياة مليئه بالوفره ... مليئه بكل ماتطلب نفسك .. فقط .. إحتفظ بما تملك .. وإنظر لما حولك ... إبحث تفكر .. راقب .. وستجد الكثير والكثير . .

أما القوه الحقيقيه فهي القبـــــول ولكــــــن وفقا لمبادئنا ...(وفقاً لمبادئك)هنا تكمن الصعوبه .فهي تعني

القوة للقبول والتعامل مع هذا الواقع وتطويع هذا الواقع لما يناسب مبادئي ... دون(القبول) انت ضعيف ..وسوف تكون عرضه للكسر بسهوله . وسوف تتوقف لفترة من الوقت ... أو في الحد الأدنى يمكن أن تضيع لفترة من الوقت ....لأنك غاضب ..أو منزعج .. وهذا الإنزعاج يجعلك تخسر مالديك من النعم ... (لماذا ؟!).. أو كيف يجعلني أخسر مالدي من النعم !؟

لأنك ببساطه لن تستشعر النعم التي لديك بعد الآن .... ليس لديك قبول أي ليس لديك إستشعار للأشياء الجميله التي تملكها . . والتي هي أصلا في حوزتك . ....

لايوجد شخص في هذا العالم لايملك أشياء جميله .. مهما كانت بسيطه .. لذلك اكرر على جلب البهجه والحب لما تفعل سواء كان عمل أو علاقة .. أنت بجلب البهجه تحافظ على مالديك تمسكه .. ويوما بعد يوم يزيد رصيد النعم عندك ... كأنك تضع في حصاله النقود المعدنيه الصغيرة ..فهي يوما بعد يوم تزداد .. وتصبح بعد فترة ما مبلغاً وقدره .

كذلك النعم البسيطه أو ماتملكه أو ماجاءك بطريقه تلقائيه كعمل أو زواج أو دراسه وتقبلته وحافظت عليه (بينما هو لايرضي طموحك) لكنك تستمر في تقبله وتحاول جلب البهجه فيه وتحاول تحسينه .. فهذا يزيد رصيدك يوماً بعد يوم .. يزيد رصيدك من الثقه بالنفس .. ويزيد رصيدك بقدرتك على مواجهه الصعوبات .وإيجاد الحلول .

قبـــــولك يزيد فرصـــــتك لتقبل المزيد من الفرص السانحه ... فالقبول هو فتح الباب للمزيد والمزيد من الفرص .

والرفض كأنك أقـــفـــلت الباب أمام الفرص السانحه .. فتتحول الى شحه .. وندرة .. بينما الأصل هو الوفره والنماء .

فهذا هو الضعف بحد ذاته... وهذا ضعف لأنك يمكن أن تذوب في محيطك لأنك أقفلت باب الفرص ورفضت واقعك .. فستبقى في محلك .. أو في نفس المستوى الذي وصلت له ... وعدم القبول .. أو القبول مع اليأس .. معناه أنك ذبت في واقعك ... وفقدت أهليتك للأنجاز وللتقدم في الحياة

وهذا من أصعب مايمكن للإنسان أن يقع فيه .. لأن حياته ستقف عند هذا الحد .

بينما يمكنني أن أسميها (القـــــــوة بحد ذاتها)إذا كنت تقبل هذا الواقع وتتعامل معه بحب وفقا لمبادئك وتطوعه وتستمر فيه للإنجاز وللتقدم بطريقه سلسه سهله وبطريقه وفقاً لما يأتي اليك بشكل طبيعي تلقائي

And why compassion and friendliness..... Because compassion and friendliness help to accept ... (Acceptance) gives you a longer breath in dealing with the obstacles

In fact you compassionate to yourself

I do not like you to leave immediately what bothers you.... Give yourself the chance to find something better first.... Take advantage of the opportunity, that you already have that job or that relationship or whatever.

(A bird in your hand is better than ten on the tree) ....even If the trees are many...and even If you are good hunter.

You don't need to push yourself into difficulties. Keep all your blessings potential and continue to search for the best.

Continuing to search for the best, gives you a wide range of options ... In addition to what you already own... (What came to you in a natural way and automatic).

Accept...... (Acceptance)... And search for the best ... Life is full of wide options ... And life is full of abundance... Full of all what you may asking yourself... Just keeping what you have... And notice the graces around you ... Think... Watch... And you will find many and many of Opportunities

The true power is acceptance, but according to our principles ... (according to your principles) here lies the difficulty

The force of acceptance and adapt to reality to fit my principles ... without (acceptance) Easy to break.... You may stop for a while ... or at the minimum may be lost for a while.... Because you are angry... or upset... and this discomfort makes you lose your blessings ... (why?!) or how could I lose my blessings?

Because you simply will not feel the grace that you have anymore.... You do not accept any sense for the beautiful things you own. .. Which is originally in your possession. ...

There is no one in this world do not have beautiful things... No matter how simple... So I repeat to bring joy and love for what you do, whether work or relationship...,... As if you Put money every day in your wallet... Day by day will increasing... And after a period becomes big sum...

Simple blessings that you has, or what you already own, and accepted it and maintained it, (while it does not satisfy your ambition) but you continue to accept and try to bring the joy and try to improve it... Increases your balance of self-confidence. Your balance increases your ability to face difficulties and find solutions.

.... أنت هنا مهيئ للأنجاز والفرح والبهجه كل يوم .

لذلك هو معنى دقيق جدا عليك أن تكون حذرا جداً إذا كنت ترغب في المضي قدما إلى الأمام وتحقيق الإنجاز يوما بعد يوم دون توقف.

(القبول وفقاً لمبادئك) .

Your acceptance increases your opportunity to accept more opportunities ... acceptance is opening the door to more and more opportunities.

And the refusal as if you shut the door to the opportunity. That will Turns to scarcity.... While the origin is prosperity and achievement.

This is weakness in itself ... This is a weakness because you can melt in your surroundings, because you closed the door of opportunities, and rejected your reality. You will remain in your level... Or at the same level that reached it

Non acceptance... Or acceptance with despair... Mean you melted in your reality ... and lost your eligibility for achievement and progress in life

And this is one of the most difficult things for a person to be stuck.in it... Because his life will stop at this point.

While I can call it (the power by itself) if you accept this reality and dealt with it according to your principles and continue to achieve and progress in a smooth and easy way and according to what comes to you naturally

....Here you are ready to achievement. And happiness each day

So it is very precise meaning you have to be very careful if you want to go ahead and achieve the day-to-day accomplishment non-stop.

(Acceptance according to your principles)..

MAKE THE FLEXIBILITY AND YOUR ACCEPTANCE ACCORDING TO YOUR PRINCIPLES

SUHAIR ALHASAN

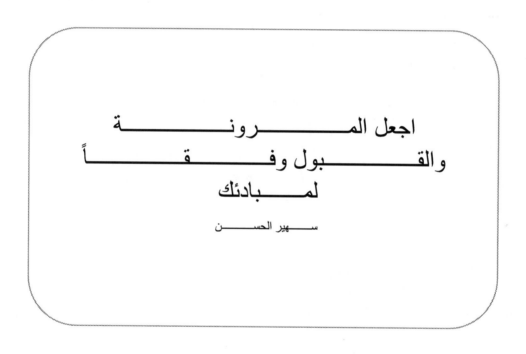

اجعل المـــــــرونـــــة
والقـــبول وفــــــقـــــاً
لمـــبادئك

سـهير الحسـن

2-TIME MANAGEMENT AND IT IMPACT ON EVERY LIFE'S DETAIL AND THE STRENGTH OF THIS FACTOR IN THE ACHIEVEMENT OF GOALS:-

Time is one of the most difficult factors to be controlled. And with that great importance and unlimited impact on the life of the individual ... it's hard to control

Because most people do not give this factor the importance that deserves

So often life pulled them to be far away from their beginning ... so often starts the individual in his life to set goals and fights for it... The fighting here is the determination and persistence to achieve this goal, and playing in the factor (time) and an adapted for benefit Considered as one of the most accurate and hardest battles at all.

Because the more time passes without Waiver you're a goal (steadfastly insisting on achieving this goal) ... the battle is still in your side

So you can do whatever you want (according to your principles) to create situation that will helps you to maintain your morale to achieve the goal ... without allowing the difficulties of life, stealing your desire to pursue achieve goals

Bring the joy and happiness to what you doing...

Or perhaps you need to give up some things in order to achieve your goal...

Or you decide to engage in spiritual activities

Or increase your knowledge... And other ways that help you to continue. ... These ways like a fast steps take you physically and spiritually to pursuing your goals.

So it is one of the most difficult battles at all... Most often find people setting their goals at the beginning of their lives ... But they often stop halfway on goals smaller than they planned in their beginnings.

Why?

Because the difficulties of life deprived them of their desire to achieve their great goal ... or they were lost in the midst of chaos or they became within the goals of others....

Here playing in time factor will create your atmosphere to keep your pursuing without boredom and non-stop

2- إدارة الوقت وتأثيره على كل تفاصيل الحياة وقوة هذا العامل في تحقيق الأهداف:-

الوقت من اهم العوامل التي يصعب التحكم فيها ومع اهميته البالغه وتأثير الغير محدود على حياة الفرد يصعب

التحكم به لان معظم الناس لايعطون هذا العامل الاهميه التي يستحق فتجرفهم الحياة تدريجياً ليكونوا بعيدين كل البعد عن مابدأو به مشوارهم ... لذلك في الغالب يبدأ الفرد في حياته بوضع اهداف ويحارب من اجلها ..المحاربه هنا هي الاصرار والثبات على تحقيق هذا الهدف.

لذلك يعتبر اللعب بعامل الوقت وتطويعه لصالحك من اكثر المعارك دقه وقوه على الاطلاق .لأنه كلما مــــر الوقت دون تنازلك عن هدفك ... اي (ثابت بإصـــرار على تحقيــق هذا الهدف) ... فالمعركه لاتزال لصالحك.

لذلك يمكنك ان تفعل ماتشاء (وفقاً لمبادئك) لتخلق لنفسك جواً يساعدك على الاحتفاظ بمعنوياتك مرتفعه لتحقيق الهدف. دون أن تسمح لصعوبات الحياة مهما كانت .. أن تسلبك هذه الاراده في تحقيقه

كأن تجلب البهجه والسعاده لما تفعل ..أو ربما تحتاج للتنازل عن بعض الاشياء في سبيل تحقيق هدفك ...أو أنك تقرر أن تزاول نشاطات روحيه ونشاطات تزيد بها ثوابك أو روحانياتك أو علمك .. وغيرها من السبل التي تعينك على الاستمرار . فهذه السبل تخطو بك بدنياً وروحانياً ... فيكون سعيك إنطـــــــــلاقاً.

لذلك هي من أصعب المعارك على الاطلاق .. ولذلك تجد الناس بالغالب يضعون أهداف في بدايه حياتهم ... ولكنهم غالباً مايتوقفون في منتصف الطريق عند أهداف اصغر مما خططوا له في بداياتهم

لماذا ؟

لأن صعوبات الحيـاة سلبتهم الرغبه في تحقيق هدفهم الكبير ... أو أنهم ضاعوا في خضم الفوضى أو صاروا ضمن اهداف الآخرين . مثلاً من يريد ترك السكائر أو من يريد إنقاص وزنه هو يعمل لفترة من الزمن بالمحافظه على التمارين الرياضيه والنظام الغذائي وغيرها من الامور المدرجه في خطه وضع هذا الهدف ..

ولكنه سرعان مايمل ويياس .. وحتى إذا لم يياس ووصل الى مبتغاه ... هو لايجب أن يتوقف .. لانه بتوقفه سيرجع الى ماكان عليه .. فهنا اللعب بعامل الوقت سيخلق لك الأجواء التي تجعلك تحافظ على مسيرتك دون ملل ودون توقف.

يعني مُنظِّـم الوقت .. ليس لديه وقت يمل فيه ... لأنه مشغول طوال الوقت ... وحتى وقت راحته هو مدرج ضمن جدول تنظيم الوقت .. يرتاح ... يعيد النشاط ... للمواصله ... أي كأنك تحتال على نفسك كي تقودها الى ماتريد.

تنظيم الوقت .. هو بعباره أخرى قياده لرغباتك نحو ماتريد ..أي نحــو هدفــك فجدول الوقت .. كل فترة اعد تنظيمه ... هو في غايه الأهميه لمن أراد ان يواصل .. تستطيع تغييره كل فترة تبعاً للفرص والنشاطات المتاحه أو التي تختلقها أنت لمواصله مسيرك .. وسترى نفسك بتقدم مستمر من حيث لاتشعر .. سبحان الله!

فهو سلاح ذو حدين .. اذا استخدمته يسير بك دون توقف نحو ماتريد .. وان اهملته دفعك بعيداً عن طريق هدفك وعلى قدر تحكمك به .. تكون سرعتك في المسير في تخطي العقبات

ولذلك بطريقه أو بأخرى (تنظيم الوقت) يعمل معك على عده أصعده ويدفعك للسعي بشتى الطرق الى الأمام بإتجاه الإنجازات (الدنيويه والروحيه) في حياتك فلاتفوت هذه الفرصة وهذا الحافز الرائع الذي يدعى (**تنظيم الوقت**)

وقد سبق وأن ذكرت أن الحياة مثل لعبه قطع كل ما كنت ماهراً في إستغلال الدقائق لخدمتك فإنك تحرز تقدم في الحياة

The person who managed his time... He does not have time to feel bored... because he is busy all the time ... even the time of rest already setting in his schedule... Relax ... Restores activity ... To continue ... As if you deceive yourself to guide it to the goal

Because you all the time has a desires, most of that desires is a way of your goal, so you have to be careful.

And (The organization of time)... Is driving your desires towards what you want... Towards your goal.

The schedule of time... Each period you must organizing your schedule ... it is for those who wanted to continue... You can change it every period depending on the opportunities and

Activities that available, you continue to progress

It is a double-edged sword. If you use it, it will pushing you nonstop towards what you want. If you neglect it, you will be pulling away from your goal.

So it's depend on controlling it, your speed in pursuit depend on the speed of overcome the obstacles. And time management one of things that helps you to overcome the obstacles

Thus, you are in one way or another (time management) work with you on several ways to going ahead towards the achievements (mundane and Spirituality) in your life, so don't miss this opportunity and this wonderful motive

It's called (time management)

I have already said that life is like a puzzle pieces. Everything you skillful in exploiting the minutes to serve you, .it will be progress in life

(TIME MANAGEMENT) DRIVING YOUR DESIRES TOWARDS WHAT YOU WANT...TOWARDS YOUR GOAL

[SUHAIR ALHASAN]

إدارة الوقـت هو قيادة لرغباتك نحو ماتريد تحقيقه
..أي قيادة لرغباتك نحو هدفــــــك

(سهير الحسـن)

(2.1) THE BEGINNING:-

Put your paper and pen and organize your time from the first minute of waking up from sleep until the time of your sleep in the evening

Hour by hour

Ex: - table (1)

Day and date	Time	The activities	Notice
Sat 10/ 25	8:00 am -9:00am	workout	
	9:00am-10am	Breakfast- pray	
	10am-12pm	homework	
	12pm-2pm	Prayer + dinner + map	
	2pm- 4pm	Reading	

Thus continue until the end of the day

This table is considered the beginning... Try to continue it... Because it helps you to monitor yourself ... and monitor your actions ... When you review weekly will show you clearly the achievement accomplished during the week (such as losing weight and the Commitment to exercises ... Or prayer or read, and the extent of your commitment to the performance on time... Or... It will be easy to note weaknesses or shortcomings in your day

This table helps you to commitment ... and to control your action ... and you will find yourself moving away from wasting time automatically... Later, it will be very hard for you waste time... Because you have used to a certain style of high-level performance during your day...

In any circumstance it will be very difficult for you to lose time or to be low performance ... and this is a catalyst... Because you will create new things... And new activities to fill your time...

So

Organize your time... Helps convert you to creative person... And to useful person at the very least.

(2-1) البــــدايـــــه :-

ضع ورقه وقلم ونظم وقتك من اول دقيقه من استيقاظك من النوم الى وقت ان يحين موعد نومك في المساء

ساعه بساعه واليك جدول توضيحي

(جــدول رقم 1)

الملاحظات	النشاط	الوقت	اليوم والتاريخ
	رياضه	8ص-9ص	السبت 2017 /10/25
	صـــلاة الضــحى وقـــراءه ورد مــن القـــرآن وافطار	9ص-10ص	
	تنظيف وطبخ	10ص-12ظ	
	صلاة وغداء وقيلوله	12.3ظ- 2:0ظ	

وهكذا تستمر حتى نهايه اليوم

هذا الجدول يعتبر البدايه .. تحاول الاستمرار عليه ..لانه يساعدك على مراقبه نفسك ... ومراقبه افعالك ... وعند مراجعته اسبوعياً سوف يظهر لك جلياً الإنجاز الذي انجزته خلال الاسبوع .(كإنقاص الوزن وانتظامك على هذا الجدول يساعدك على الالتزام ... والانظباط ... وستجد نفسك تبتعد عن إضاعه الوقت أوتوماتيكياً .. لا بل لاحقاً سيكون من الصعب جداً عليك إضاعه الوقت .. لإنك قد إعتدت على نمط معين من الاداء العالي المستوى خلال يومك .

فتحت أي ظرف من الظروف سيكون من الصعب عليك جداً اضاعه الوقت أو أن تكون فرد منخفض الأداء ... وهذا عامل محفز .. لإنك حينما تضطر لسبب ما أن تتوقف عن فعل معين أو إلتزام معين فإنك ستختلق أشياء جديده .. ونشاطات جديده مفيده لتملأ بها وقتك ..

لذلك

تنظيم الوقت .. يرتقي بك الى فرد عالي الأداء اي فرد مبدع وخلاق .. أو مفيد في اقل تقدير.وهو من أدق الطرق التي تساعدك على التعود على التنظيم ومراقبه الإنجاز في حياتك ... بل تعد طريقه تفكيرك لتتفكير بطريقه جديده مختلفه تماماً عما كنت عليه .

سوف تلاحظ بنفسك كيف تتغير ذاتك ..... مع مواصلتك على إعداد هذا الجدول ...

(2.2) TIME OF RECREATION

Fancy that being a committed person and having a vision and goal that you do not care about the recreation and I have to be dismal person, and this is very wrong

Do not let your daily schedule of times lack of self-recreation, for example hiking... Or reading. Or visiting friends...

Even have to have a certain time, you can sit in it without any responsibilities... It is your own time. This time is considered a time to restore activity to the brain and to the body and to the mental state

. It is a time devoid of responsibilities, this time out is important because it is an important factor in maintaining and continuing to strive to achieve the goal ... This time may be taken either daily or weekly depending on the schedule that you follow

The importance of this factor is also that it maintains your social relationships that you cannot live without it, you are a social by being instinctively... That is, God Almighty did to us

Some people in the midst of responsibilities and pursuit of goals is busy all the time and forgets his duties towards family or parents ... and even forgets his duties towards himself.

You need to rest ... need to stop for a moment to ask.... You need this time to enjoy the simple things that you own and sometimes not noticed in the midst of this hectic race in life

Opening your eyes at the end of the race is the worst things in the hearts of human beings. This feelings is often felt by the father who is dedicated to building the future of his family and work and forgetting himself or the mother who forgot herself in the responsibilities of raising children ... or wealthy man that made his fortune at the expense of the most beautiful days of his life.

If the time passed and the great man felt that he lost his age, beautiful times... And wonderful things passed and he did not feel it. It will never return.

So times of recreation have more dimensions than you imagine.

In addition to this ... These times make the family members close to each other at a time has become family bonding is not possible

You May ask a question that how can family relate to achieve the goals?

It is one of the most important questions raised in this matter.

(2-2) الــــوقـــــات وأوقــــــات النــــزهة أو التـــــرويــــح عــــن النــــفـــــس

البعض قد يتوهم بأن كوني شخص ملتزم ولدي رؤيه وهدف أني لا أهتم بالنزه ,أو يستهين بالترويح عن النفس وهذا شئ خاطئ جدا

لايجب أن يخلو جدولك اليومي من أوقات مخصصه للترويح عن الذات مثلاً التنزه .. أو القراءه .. أو زياره الأصدقاء ..

لا بل لابد من وجود وقت معين تستطيع أن تجلس فيه بدون أي مسؤليات ..إنه وقتك الخاص . هذا الوقت يعتبر وقتاً لإعاده النشاط الى الدماغ والى الجسم وللحاله النفسيه على حد سواء

هو وقت خالي من المسؤوليات . وهذا الوقت المستقطع أهميته تكمن في أنه سبب مساعد على المداومه والاستمرار في السعي لتحصيل الهدف ...قد يكون هذا الوقت المستقطع إما يومياً أو اسبوعياً تبعاً للجدول المتبع .

تكمن أهمية هذا العامل أيضا أنه يحافظ على علاقاتك الأجتماعية التي لاتستطيع الحياة بدونها فأنت كائن إجتماعي بالفطرة .. أي أن الله عز وجل جعل لك هذه الصفه

فالبعض في خضم المسؤوليات والسعي لتحقيق اهدافه يكون مشغولاً طوال الوقت وينسى واجباته تجاه العائله أو الوالدين ... وينسى حتى واجباته تجاه نفسه

فنفسه تحتاج للراحه ... تحتاج للتوقف لوهله عن التسائل والاستنتاج .... تحتاج لهذا الوقت للتمتع بالاشياء البسيطه التي تملكها والتي لاتلاحظها أحياناً في خضم هذا السباق المحموم في الحياة

ففتح عينيك في نهايه السباق من أكثر الأشياء التي تثير الحسرة في قلوب البشر ..وهذا الشعور غالباً مايشعر به الأب المتفاني في بناء مستقبل عائلته وعمله ونسي نفسه أو الأم التي نسيت نفسها في خضم مسؤوليات تربيه الأبناء ... أو العصامي الذي كون ثروته على حساب أجمل أيام عمره .

فإذا مرّ الوقت وكبرالإنسان شعر بأنه فقد من عمره أوقات جميله ..وأشياء رائعه مرت ولم يشعر بها . ولن تعود أبداً .

لذلك كانت أوقات النزه لها أبعاد أكثر مما تتصور أنت .

بالإضافه الى ذلك ... هذه الأوقات تقرب المسافه بين أبناء العائله الواحده في وقت أصبح الترابط الأسري معدوم .. وقد يسأل سائل ماعلاقه الترابط الأسري بتحقيق الاهداف ؟!

وهو من أهم الأسئله التي تطرح في هذا الموضوع ..

لأن الترابط الأسري قطعه من قطع لعبه البزل التي تبني حياة مستقرة وفرد قوي قادر على الأنجاز وتحقيق الأهداف .. وبدونه أنت تدور في حلقه مفرغه ... وإن كان يبدو لك انك تتقدم .....

Because the family one of the puzzle pieces, that build a stable life and a strong individual is able to achieve goals... Without it you are weak ... even if it seems like progress....

Because if you lose this factor, as if you put the money in a pierced bag.... Day after day and under your engagement to your pursuing goals you will lose your relationship with whom you love and this is very bad.

Because when you continue to collect goals will face the times that you need who around you... And sometimes who around you needs your attention, you must be available to them.

Having someone you love around you is a motivational factor for you ... take care of it.

Get out of the anxiety that may control the human when you face a difficulty, where you cannot reach a solution

Science says that if you restrict yourself to this dilemma you cannot overcome it, but if you give it your back ... I mean, forget all the subject completely... Do not think about it... you can easy find a solution...... And the recreation here is one of the most beautiful things that help you

Recreation time is preserves virtue in society ... in light of the modern era and its operations ... and the many bad things that may tempt the human. Or tempt your children ... You get used to the times of the family picnic ... As if you are protect your children ... You are in an indirect way give them this immunity against the fear that your son falls in ...

The times of fun is the most beautiful things that help you to immunize yourself and your family... And expand your work in a safe way....

Without daily or weekly picnic times ... it will be difficult to pursue the right path towards achieving new goals day after day.

لانك إذا فقدت هذا العامل فكأنك تضع المحصول في كيس مثقوب ....يوما بعد يوم وفي ظل انهماكك ستفقد علاقتك بمن تحب وهذا سئ جداً

لأنك في مواصلتك لتحصيل الأهداف ستواجه أوقات تحتاج فيها لمن حولك .. وأوقات ما من حولك يحتاجون لك لابد أن تكون متواجد لهم.

وجود من تحب حولك هو عامل دافع لك ... محفز لك .... لابد من الإحتفاظ به

النزهة تخرجك من حالة القلق الذي قد يسيطر على الأنسان عندما تواجهك مشكله صعبه لاسمح الله أو صعوبه ما لاتستطيع الوصول فيها الى حل

والعلم الحديث يقول أنك إذا واجعتك معضله ما أو شعور سئ لازمك   أنت لاتستطيع تجاوزه إلا إذا ادرت له ظهرك .. أي بمعنى تنسى الموضوع تماما .. لاتفكر فيه ... والنزهه هنا من أجمل الأشياء التي تعينك على ذلك

النزهة تحافظ على الفضيلة في المجتمع ... في ظل العصر الحديث ومجرياته ... وتعدد الأشياء السيئه التي قد تغري الأنسان أو تغري أبناءك . المراهقين ... فأنت بالتعود على أوقات النزهة العائليه ... كأنك تحفظ ابناءك ...أنت بطريقه غير مباشره تعطيهم هذه المناعه ضد ماتخاف أن يقع فيه إبنك ...

فأوقات النزهة من أجمل الأشياء التي تعينك على تحصين نفسك وعائلتك .. وتوسع مداك لتعمل بطريقه آمنه ... .

بدون أوقات النزهة اليوميه أو الأسبوعيه ... سيكون من الصعب السعي على الطريق الصحيح الثابت الخطى نحو تحقيق اهداف جديده يوما بعد يوم .

SECTION 4
THE TOOLS OF PURSUING GOALS

الفصـــــل الرابع
أدوات تحقــــيق الأهـــــداف

1-BRING HAPPINESS AND JOY IN ALL WHAT YOU DOING: _

Bringing happiness and joy to all what you do is an important factor helping you to make progress in your life ... (the joy) makes your energy renewed... You enjoying to be around optimistic person.so you can be that person, Scientists said ((Who practice satisfaction would be satisfied)) ... And always had accomplished during his day. Much more than who doesn't brought the joy to his life.

A man who knows how to bring the joy and happiness to what he doing, nothing can stopping his pursuit achieve goals or his daily achievements

That person having a vision, and his reacting to what happens around him could be cool and positive. He is optimistic. It is not emotional. (He doesn't follow his feeling, but logic analysis to understanding what going on surrounding him)

Positive neutrality is what helps a person who is optimistic in his interaction with what happening in his surrounding ... despair shouldn't know his way... If you want to achieve goals day after day non-stop.

(...Bring joy and happiness) for all what you doing considered to additional power to help you move forward.

Joy and happiness helps to indulge in the work and enjoy it and this makes you fully linked to what you do ... It keeps you away from the boredom... And makes you more innovative in your work and more proficient ... Hence the focus on this factor is so important in our life.

You adapt your surroundings in a diplomatic way, to be in your serve, and therefore you are indulge with your current moment, and therefore you are faster to getting your aims.

Bringing joy makes you active and younger in pursuing your goal. It's just motive that's you need to do for a period of time to keep your energy high. ... To overcoming the obstacles that you could face ... or to overcoming bad feelings that you could feel for this reason or that

Focus on how I bring joy ... will help to be present ... here and now ... this in itself is great ... because it is very important that no one can control my mood or my mind while I am totally connected to What I am doing ... my work will be perfect because I focused on it ... Give all my attention ... I do my best in it.

Bringing joy to what I am doing helps me to continue my work longer ... because I have maintained my energy high ... without boredom

1- الرضــا و جـــلــب الســـعادة أو البـــهـجه في كـــل ماتـفـــعل :-

يعتبر جلب السعاده والبهجه الى كل ماتفعله عامل مهم في مساعدتك على احراز التقدم في والإنجاز في حياتك ... فالأبتهاج يجعل طاقتك متجدده ,, ونفسك طيبه ..قال العلماء ((من رضي فله الرضا)) والراضي أو السعيد تجده إنسان ذو طاقه عاليه تحب أن تكون بجانبه ... ويكون دائما منجز خلال يومه .أكثر بكثير من الأنسان المحبط او الكئيب ...

الانسان الذي يعرف كيف يجلب السعاده الى مايفعل تجده نادراً مايتوقف في سعيه لاحراز اهدافه او في إنجازاته اليوميه ...

وكذلك تجده إنسان ينظر الى الأمور من بُعـــــد فهـــو لايتفاعل بالأحداث .لذلك هو متفائل .. وهو ليس إنفعالي .

الحياد الايجابي هو مايساعد الإنسان المتفائل في تفاعله مع الأحداث ...فلايجب أن يعرف اليأس طريقك .. إذا كنت ممن يرغب بتحقيق أهداف يوما بعد يوم بدون توقف

(الرضا ... وجلب البهجه والسعاده) لكل ماتفعل .. فهذه قوة اضافيه تساعدك على المضي قدماً.

الأبتهاج والسعاده تساعد على الإنغماس في العمل والتمتع فيه وهذا مرتبط كلياً في ماتفعل ... فهو يبعدك عن الشرود والملل .. ويجعلك اكثر إبتكاراً في عملك واكثر إتقاناً ... التركيز على كيفية جلب الفرح ... سوف تساعد على أن تكون موجود ... هنا والآن ... وهذا في حد ذاته إنجاز عظيم ... لأنه من المهم جدا أن لا أحد يستطيع السيطرة على مزاجي أو ذهني بينما أنا تماما متصلا ما أقوم به ... عملي سيكون مثاليا لأنني أركز فيه ومرتبط فيه ... أعط كل ما عندي من الاهتمام ... أبذل قصارى جهدي في ذلك....

فأنا أعمل بحريه ... أنطلق في سعيي لاشئ يقيدني ... لا ظروف , ولا عوائق ,, ولا عقبات .

جلب الفرح إلى ما أفعله يساعدني على مواصلة عملي لمدة أطول ... لأنني حافظت على طاقتي عالية ... دون الملل انها الخروج من أي طاقة سلبية ... أو أفكار سلبية حملتها ممكن ان تؤثر علي .

من جهة أخرى الرضا وجلب البهجه والسعاده لحياتك هي نوع من تحقيق الذات بالأشياء المتاحه حولك .. هي نوع من تقدير النعم حولك ... والعلماء قالوا الشكر قيد النعم ..فحتى تتمكن من المضي قدماً لابد لك من الإحتفاظ بماتملك ... فإذا فقدت هذا التقدير أو الإستماع بما تملك .. فقدت تحقيق ذاتك .. سوف تكون منسلخ عن محيطك ودائرتك ... ستكون في عزله ... وهي من أسوأ أنواع العزله على الإطلاق أن يكون الإنسان في عزله عن ذاته ..حيث تكون العزله عن ذاته كإنسان محب للعيش .. والتحقيق والإنجاز .. وهكذا .. ستجد نفسك مرتبك .. مكسور ... وضعيف ... ويزداد ضعفك يوم بعد يوم .. فترى البعض عصبي المزاج ... منزعج في أغلب يومه ... لايجد الرضا او الراحه في محيطه ... هو يبحث عن شئ غير موجود .. يركز على الغائب ويهمل مايملك .. يهمل نقط قوته ..لاتجعل نفسك بهذا الموقف قدر المستطاع ..

وبنفس الوقت أحب ان اقول لك لو كنت صاحب طموح عالي فإنك بكل الأحوال ستتعرض لنوع من العزله .. انها حاله ايجابيه واجباريه فيمن ينظر للبعيد ... لكن دعني اقول اني أضيئ لك الطريق .. واحذرك من أن تجعل نفسك في عزلة مضاعفه أنت في غنى عنها .. الحياة مليئه بالفرص ومجتمعك زاخر بأنواع النعم والملذات المباحه .. الله سبحانه وتعالى جعلك مخلوق اجتماعي ... لأنك هنا لسبب ألا وهو إعمار الأرض ... أي التقدم والإنجاز ... ولهذه المهمه جعل لك مساعدة ومن ضمن هذه المساعدة المجتمع.. وماحولك ... لذلك استخدم

It's getting out of any negative energy ... or any negative thoughts I've carried.

You can notice how much (bringing the joy to what you do) and its impact on your work, your productivity ... and the mood.

On the other hand, the satisfaction and bring joy and happiness to your life is a kind of self-realization with the things available around you... It is a kind of appreciation of the blessings around you ... The scientists said the gratitude can be reason for keep your blessings. ... If lost this appreciation or enjoyment of what you have... You will Lost your real-self... You will be detached from your surroundings and your circle ... You will be isolated ... It is one of the worst types of isolation at all to be a person in isolation from himself... You will find yourself confused... Broken... And weak ... And increase your weakness day after day ... nervous mood... Troubled in most of his day ... No satisfaction or rest in his surroundings ... He is looking for something away than his presence of... Concentrates on the absent and neglecting what he have... Neglecting his strengths ... The fact that you achieve yourself (appreciation of the blessings around you ... by integrating with your surroundings) you impose yourself on your reality and vent yourself to move to the next level of your life... For Any new achievement. ..

It can be said to the owner of the high ambition ... that his (satisfaction) is the case of easy abstain ... difficult to achieve and to dwell in it ... because you are trying to stand on your land or space available, which feel that it is too small for you .. Because your ambition appeals to you, but attracts you strongly and almost make you fall ... The isolation is often the enemy of the owner of high ambition... Because you must balance between the facts of your reality on the one hand and the data of your ambition and access to it on the other hand ... This balance difficult to achieve ... because you are forced to accept things that may be less than your ambition...... Here you must restrict yourself to your reality by appreciate what you own firstly and secondly Raise the ceiling of your ambitions to move to the next level In the ladder of your success ... depending on your determination.. Because despair and isolation will be your enemy ... Many stands ... and broken ambition ... Refraction of ambition is the first step in retreat ... And loss of satisfaction ... is the first stage in the loss of your property.

If you lost ambition and lost your strength by belonging to your surroundings... And investigate yourself and lost this insistence on existence and progress ... Become a broken man... Not happy ... And have no hope... I do not think that any person prefer this feeling instead of happiness and achievement and success and excellence in life.

So satisfaction ... or brought joy one of the most precise factors that must be focused on it ... while keeping the ceiling of your ambition high ... regardless of your reality... Or the data of your current life.

Enjoy all that is available to you from the fairly permissible graces that God has mocked for you ... as a force that helps you accomplish ... as a force to rise. As a force to self-affirmation ... Yourself as a strong and successful man... He deals with the data of life defiantly and prudently... Beyond all obstacles and difficulties.

هذه النعمه .. اندمج .. اجلب البهجه .. تحرك .. لكن بدون الذوبان في المجمتع .. بدون أن تنسى أهدافك واحلامك التي تريد انجازها استخدم نعمة جلب البهجة والسعادة كعامل مساعد وليس كهدف لأنه في الحقيقه ان السعادة الحقيقيه في تحقيق الأهداف وفي الأنجاز والتقدم .

كلما كنت خياراتك اكثر في جلب البهجه والسعادة والفرح المباح الى حياتك .. كلما كنت أقوى في التقدم نحو أنجازاتك .. وأهدافك .

A person who longs for progress in his life never look at his reality and is not affected by what is around him no matter what he aspires to because he builds the reality that he wants in his imagination... Plan it ... Draws... Feel it.... Then brings his plans to reality. With every step of his life he strives towards progress in the way of achievements. And that is the beauty of this life.

2-AMPLIFY SATISFACTION BY FOCUSING ON SELF-SATISFACTION

The scholars say (who seek of satisfied will owning it) is a great saying.. If you focused on its meaning, you find that the space of satisfaction will increases by amplify the feeling of the satisfaction in your life ... and the satisfaction does not come by the material things around you, but satisfaction feeling emanating from the soul .. It's a decision that you have to take. This feeling is which takes you to a higher level... Or to another achievement in life, but the beginning is from you... The initiative is from you...

This factor is linked to the previous point and the satisfaction and bring joy... Because it is a golden rule.... It has ancient origins in our culture... Did not come by the way.

Build a base for yourself... How? ... By appreciation what you have... By

Integration into your surroundings.....your surroundings ... Does your surroundings have any effect (if you like that surroundings or not) ..?!

I answer you no!

A sense of satisfaction is a decision you take... Regardless of your surroundings... Whatever your circumstances... Whatever the difficulties that stand in your way ... Your ability to deal with this reality... Or obstacles are a kind of creating an area that you can stand on it... And as much as the Satisfaction and acceptance of reality and the environment and obstacles is more.... The more you can deal with this reality and the obstacles flexibly... And strongly...

Which will increase your strength on the Skip obstacles and make them at your service... Instead of being a reason to stop you or break your ambition...

And since it is a personal decision which you want from yourself, you want satisfaction. And you want to accept this situation, that is, to give yourself the order to acceptance ... The amplification of satisfaction will be what you have to do to push yourself to comply with this decision. ... You are starting to lead yourself towards what you want.

In general, the human nature has common points that can be focused on and enjoyed by it, such as family, leisure and recreation ... or even taking a day off when it is free of any Responsibilities.. As well as rituals and religious rituals are things that enter tranquility and warmth to the human spirit.. The focus on these activities and others.. Is to serve the human... To give us the strength and motivation for achievement, progress and giving...

2- جلب البهجة والسعادة المباحة وتحقيق الذات :-

. الحقيقه أنك بتحقيق ذاتك (بتقدير النعم حولك ... بالإندماج بمحيطك) انت تفرض نفسك على واقعك وتهئ نفسك للإنتقال الى المستوى التالي من حياتك .. اي الى إنجاز جديد ...

يمكن أن يقال لصاحب الطموح العالي ... أن حاله (الرضا) عنده هو حاله من السهل الممتنع ... يصعب تحقيقها والإتزان فيها ... لأنك تحاول أن تقف على أرضك أو مساحتك المتاحه التي تحس انها صغيرة جداً لتسعك .. لأن طموحك يناديك بل يجذبك بقوة ويكاد يسقطك ... العزله واليأس في الغالب هي العدو اللدود لصاحب الطموح العالي .. لانه وجب عليك تحقيق التوازن بين معطيات واقعك ومعطيات طموحك وماتود الوصول اليه من جهة اخرى ... هذا التوازن صعب التحقيق ... لأنه يفرض عليك قبول أشياء قد تكون أقل من طموحك ...... هنا وجب عليك تقييد نفسك الطموحه الى ماتملك لتحتفظ اولا بما تملكه وثانياً حتى تنتنقل الى المستوى التالي أو الى الدرجه التالية في سلم نجاحك ... وعلى قدر اصرارك يكون الإنتقال .. لأن اليأس والعزله سيكون لك بالمرصاد ... فالكثير يقف ... وينكسر طموحه ... **إنكسار الطموح هي اول مرحله في التقهقر ... وفقدان الرضا ... هي أول مرحله في فقدان ماتملك** .

فإذا فقدت الطموح وفقدت نقط قوتك بإنتمائك لمحيطك ..وتحقيق ذاتك وفقدت هذا الإصرار على الوجود والتقدم ... أصبحت إنسان محطم .. غير سعيد ... ولايملك أي أمل .. ولا أعتقد أن اي انسان يفضل هذا الشعور على الشعور بالسعادة والإنجاز والنجاح والتفوق في الحياة .

لذلك كان الرضا ... أو جلـــب البهجه من أدق العوامـــــــــل التي وجب التركيز عليها .... مع الإحتفاظ بسقف طموحك عالي ... بغض النظر عن واقعك .. أو عن معطيات حياتك الحاليه .

استمع بكل ماهو متاح لك من النعم الحلال التي سخرها الله لك ... كقوه تساعدك على الإنجاز . كقوه على الإرتقاء . كقوة على إثبات الذات ... ذاتك كإنسان قوي ناجح .. يتعامل مع معطيات الحياة بتحدٍ وبتعقل .. يتجاوز كل العقبات والصعاب .

فالإنسان الذي يتوق للتقدم في حياته لاينظر الى واقعه ولا يتأثر بما حوله مهما كان بعيداً عن ما يطمح له لأنه يبني الواقع الذي يريده في مخيلته ..يخططه له ... يرسمه ... يشعر به .... ثم يجلب ماخطط له الى واقعه ... خطوه خطوه .. مع كل خطوه من خطوات حياته هو يسعى نحو التقدم في طريق الإنجازات . وهذه هي لذه الحياة

Use it.. Clinging to it.. Amplify the joy in it.. Respect for the time and details accurate..,. You have to make the family and allocate the time to the parents and wife and children. In fact, you devote time for yourself. You pick up your breath. These things are a kind of strength for you as a person who wants to do something in this life..

Worship as well..... ... Relationships.. And many other things are very simple elements of our daily lives.. Are the strengths of the ambitious person.... Are factors of success and progress, not goals. And we have to separate between the factors of success and the goals

جلب البهجه المباحة يعزز إنتماءك لمحيطك والإندماج فيه يعزز نقط قوتك .. يطور واقعك..تطوير واقعك يهيئك للإنتقال الى المرحله التاليه في الإنجاز والتقدم

سهـــــير الحـــــسـن

3-MEDITATION:-

Do not make your daily schedule also free of time to think this time of (meditation) even if it does not exceed ten minutes... it still very necessary

It's kind of worship. And the meditation take you to another level higher and higher in life... Organizing for all the emotions, absorbed anger or hatred... Or despair ... even grabbing happiness... Its helps to balance without counterfeiting ... You will see the obvious impact on all your behavior by yourself only after sustaining it for a period of time.

Then you will evaluating things in your own way and on a different way than other people... Its helps you to have your own vision of life.

Thinking helps you determine your goal, or what you want, or what steps will help you to progress, or who will help you to achieve your goal

It focuses your thinking on your goal... The lessons learned.... and other observation options available in front of you.

Thinking makes you think about creation and creator ... and help you to put things in their true balance, whether it is secular or spiritual.

It is a wide space for those who want to practice it...

And thinking is different than worry.... the worry make the thought and body tired ... But meditation is thinking about the causes and results and how to overcome the crisis... Do you deserve all of this or not ... And you will find yourself after meditate become more active self... As if you Escaped from constraint, It will continue your life and will probably continue your life to a better achievement than you lost because you got the science by thinking ... Do not have to try again The saying goes (learning only from self-experience) But meditate gives you the opportunity to learn without actually trying, without being exposed to this shock or Obstacle Because you got the science thinking. Look at the beauty of this tool

Unlike the anxiety that makes you restricted to this problem or the obstacle facing your path. It may stop you altogether.

3- تضخيم الرضا من خلال التركيز على الرضا الذاتي:-

يقول العلماء (من رضي فله الرضا) هي مقوله عظيمه .. لو ركزت في معناها لوجدت أن الرضا يزداد بالتضخيم والرضا لايأتي بالأشياء الماديه من حولك ولكن الرضا شعور نابع من النفس ..فإذا شعرت به ضخمه إستشعره .. حافظ عليه .. هذا الشعور هو الذي ينقلك الى مرتبه أعلى .. أو الى إنجاز آخر في الحياة تكون منك انت .. لكن البدايه تكون منك انت .. المبادرة تكون منك ..

بصراحة هي كانت بالنسبة لي نقطة تحول ... حيث اني لم اكن اعرفها او استطيع الوصول الى هذه الحالة او النقطة من التوازن .. استطيع ان اقول انه توازن .. لانه ليس كل واحد يستطيع الرضا ... بدون مقومات الرضا لديه .. فكانت تجربتي الحياتية خير مدرب لي .. وخير معلم لي .. سبحان الله .. وتعلمت وفهمت مقولة (من رضي فله الرضى) .. معنى عميق وليس سهل الوصول اليه ابداً .

هذا العامل مرتبط بالنقطه السابقه وهي الرضا وجلب البهجه .... لأنه يعتبر قاعدة ذهبيه .... لها أصول قديمه وعريقه في ثقافتنا .. ولم تأتي إعتباطاً .

ابن لنفسك قاعدة .. كيف ؟... بتقدير ماتملك .. بالاندماج بمحيطك ... هل المحيط له أي دور ..؟!

اجيبك لا !

الشعور بالرضا هو قرار أنت تتخذه .. بغض النظر عن محيطك .. ومهما كانت ظروفك .. ومهما كانت الصعاب التي تعترض طريقك ... قدرتك على التعامل مع هذا المحيط .. او العقبات هي نوع من خلق مساحه لك تقف عليها .. وكل ماكان الرضا والقبول للواقع والمحيط والعقبات .. اكبر .. كلما كان تعاملك مع هذا الواقع والعقبات مرن اكثر .. وقوي اكثر ..

أي ستزداد قوتك على ليي الصعاب وجعلها في خدمتك .. بدلاً ان تكون سبب في إيقافك أو كسر طموحك لاسمح الله .

وبما أنه قرار شخصي أي رغبه نابعه من ذاتك أنك تريد الرضا .. وأنك تريد أن تقبل هذا الوضع أي تعطي لنفسك الأمر بالقبول ... سيكون تضخيم الرضا هو ماعليك فعله لدفع نفسك على الإمتثال لهذا القرار . . أي أنك بدأت تقود نفسك نحو ماتريد .

تضخيم الرضا بمعنى التركيز على المواطن التي تجد نفسك ترتاح فيها وتسكن وتستمع ... وبصورة عامة الطبيعه البشريه لها نقاط مشتركه يمكن ان تركز عليها وتستمتع بها .. كالأسرة .. والراحه والإستجمام ... أو حتى أخذ يوم إجازة تكون فيه خالي من أية مسؤليات .. وكذلك الطقوس والشعائر الدينية هي من الأشياء التي تدخل السكينة والدفئ الى الروح البشريه .. فالتركيز على هذه الأنشطه وغيرها .. هي لخدمة الإنسان .. لتعطيه القوة والدافع على الإنجاز والتقدم والعطاء ... في خضم صعوبات الحياة وتشعباتها المختلفه .

إستخدمها .. تشبث بها .. تضخيم البهجه فيها .. باحترامها واحترام أوقاتها وتفاصيلها الدقيقه .. فإحترام الوالدين مثلاً وإيقاف جميع أشغالك لبرهما أو لزيارتهما.. أنت كإنسان طموح يريد التحقيق والإنجاز في الحياة لابد لك من هذه الأمور .. لابد لك من بر الوالدين .. لابد لك من الأسرة وتخصيص الوقت للزوجه والأولاد ..في الحقيقه أنت تخصص وقت مستقطع لك أنت ...تلتقط فيه انفاسك .. هذه الأشياء هي نقط القوة لك كإنسان يريد أن يفعل شئ في هذه الحياة .

العباده كذلك ..... والنزه أو العائله ... العلاقات .. وغيرها من الأشياء البسيطة جداً هي من عناصر حياتنا اليوميه .. هي نقاط قوة للإنسان الطموح ..هي عوامل للنجاح والتقدم وليست أهداف وهناك فرق

فالشخص الذي يكون همه أو هدفه هو الأسرة .. أو الصلاة (العبادة) .. أو غيرها من عناصر الحياة ... تراه يقف عند مستوى معين .. لابل قد لاينجح بالبتات في أي منها ...

لأن من يريد الزوجه مثلاً قد يحصل عليها ولكنه بعد فترة سوف يمل أو قد يتعرض لصعوبات في الحياة فيكون امامه خيارين أما الخوض في تجربه جديده مصيرها كمصير الأولى .. او أنه يستمر في الأولى بالرغم من تعاسته هذه التعاسه التي سوف تشغله عن التفكير في اي أهداف جديدة أو إنجاز جديد ...

وكذلك (العبادة) مثلاً فالمنقطع للعبادة ...سوف يكون إنسان أما عالة على من حوله .. يحتاج من يعيله ويصرف عليه ... أو إذا كان ميسوراً سيكون إنسان راكد منعزل .. منسلخ عن الحياة والإنجاز ... وهذه تعتبر إساءه للدين نفسه .. **لأن كل الأديان جاءت لتنظيم الحيـــــــاة وليس الركود** .... وكذلك بقيه عوامل أو كوامن القوة للإنسان الطموح .

فتضخيم الرضا والقبول والبهجه في الحياة ... مع الحفاظ على سقف طموح عالي ..... هو الدافع للتقدم والإنجاز في الحياة ...

على مستوى فرد أو على مستوى مجتمع .. وازن بين ربط نفسك بمكامن القوة لديك (بتضخيم الرضا) من جهة وبين ربط نفسك بأهداف تسعى لتحقيقها من جهة أخرى ... هو الطريق للإنجاز والتحقيق في الحياة .

بدون الرضا .. أنت تفقد قوتك يوماً بعد يوم ... وتفقد حماسك .. وتفقد رغبتك بالمواصله أخيراً ويجتاحك اليأس .

126

التـــــقدم في طريق الإنجاز في حياتك يكــون عن طريق

تضخيم مواطن الرضــا والقبول لتضخيم قوتك من جهة .... ورفع سقف أهدافـــك من جهة أخرى لحثك على السير قدماً

(سهـــير الحســـن)

4-THE MEDITATION AND THE SPECIAL GOAL:-

Meditation will help you to asking yourself (why you are here?)

Will help you to having that desire to put your fingerprint in this life.

Help you to INTENT do something before you leaving this life that cherish it.

Just intent honesty that you want to be in serve for that great universe ..... And God will guide you to achieve that **special goal.**

It is a special purpose ... You may not know how to be in the serve for this universe.... I'm sure most of you may be laughing and say [even I hardly know what my goals is!]

I tell you, I am like you, too ... But meditation moves your thinking to a higher level ... making you want to do something that has an effect

Frankly, I tell you that I was a day like you until my life was at risk because of the war.

And I just wondering

On someday All people will leave this life ... No one is immortal in it... And I felt like (I have to leave this life as I came to it ... I did not add anything to it.)

I sincerely wish that God help me and save me... And give me life ... and give me the ability to do something... and when my time to leave is coming I'll be happy with what I have done ...

I will not forget this thinking that was in my mind whenever I was in hard time.

I do not know what I can do for this world... But I do what I can in my private life... Very simple I try to achieve my own goals that do not exceed.... Repair my environment (my house) and reform myself

The great goal and I often cannot even call it a goal as much as I call it .just an idea. (Can I do something worth mentioning in this life)

Because I hate death ... but I must ... I hoped that I have achieved something before my death, makes me proud of this life that I lived.... And enjoyed it

Perhaps it is a kind of philosophy ... but it is one of the finest ideas that can take you to another level ... your interests have differed.

You always feel that you are looking and looking for what you can do.

4-التـــــفــــــــكُّــــــر

لاتجعل جدولك اليومي أيضاً يخلو من وقت للتفكر هذا الوقت حتى لو كان لايتجاوز العشر دقائق .. لكنه ضروري جداً جداً

التفكُّــر أو قوة التفكــير هو القــوة الناتجه من التفكُّــر أو التأمــــــل ..... يمكن أن نسميها (قـــوة التفكـــر) ... لأنها قــوه جبارة ... اذا استطعت أن تملكها وتتحكم بها .. سارت بك الى الأمام

ففي الدين الأسلامي مثلا ...من العبادات التي ذكرت فيه ..(عـــباده التفكُّــر) ... فهي عباده يثاب الإنسان على فعلها ... لأهميتها البالغه في بناء عقول قويه ... تملك هـــذه القــوة على التمييز وإيجاد طريقها .

فلما نزل الوحي على النبي محمد صلى الله عليه وسلم ... كان في الغار في الجبل يتعبد ... أي يمارس التفكر .... هذا التفكر .. كان بمثابه شئ تمهيدي لنزول البعثه عليه . سبحان الله

في الدين الإسلامي أيضاً هناك مايدعى بصـــلاة قيام الليل (هي الأن شبه مندثرة) .. وهي صلاة يقوم بها العبد في منتصف الليل .. بينما يكون الكل نيام .... وتُـــعد من أرقى العبادات ... حيث أن أحد منافعها الدنيويه ... تنميه قـــوة التفكـر لدى الإنسـان .

لذلك كان فقهـــــاء المسلمين في مامضى .. عندما كانوا يحافظون على هذه العباده كانوا ثاقبي الذهن .... لديهم فراسة ... وسرعه بديهه ... وقدرة على تمييز الأشياء

كذلك من يعيش في أماكن بعيده عن صخـــــب الحياة ... كالذين يعيشون في القرى .. او في الاماكن التي ليس فيها زحام ...... والذين ليس لديهم نشاط اجتماعي كثيف .... فهؤلاء يمارسون التأمل بشكل اوتوماتيكي وبشكل يومي

بالغالب تراهم بعيدين عن العشوائيه .. وتراهم منظمين ... وقدرتهم على معرفه الأشياء قويه بسبب هذا الصفاء الذهني الذي حصلوا عليه بالمداومه والتدريب على التأمل بذهن صافي

فامتلكوا قـــــوة التفكـــر تلقائياً ...

فها أنا ذا أقـــدم لك ... سـلاح آخـــر .. من أقوى الاسلحه التي تســـاعدك على تحـــقيق هدفك ... مهما كان .... بسهـــوله وسـلاســه

الا وهو (قـــــوة التفكيـــــر) أو بعبارة أخرى .. (صـفاء الذهـــــن)

فالتفكر عباده والتفكر يرقى بالفكر .. والتفكر منبه من الغفله.......منظم للنفس البشريه .....منظم لكل إنفعالاتها يمتص الغضب أو الكراهيه .. أو اليأس ... ويساعدك على جلب السعاده الى نفسك والى حياتك ....لاتستهين به أبداً .. فهو يضع لك الأمور في ميزانها الحقيقي بدون تزييف ...ولن ترى نتائجه الواضحه على نفسك إلا بعد المداومه عليه فترة من الزمن

حيث ستجد نفسك تقييم الأمور بطريقتك الخاصه وبمقياس مختلف عن الأخرين .. اي يساعدك على ان تكون لك رؤيتك الخاصه للأمور

فالتفكر عباده... والتفكر يرقى بالفكر ...
والتفكر منبه من الغفله... منظم للنفس
البشريه .....منظم لكل إنفعالاتها

(سهــــير الحســــن)

والتفكر يساعدك على تجاوز الصدمات أو الأزمات بشكل سليم ... لأنه يأخذ الأزمه التي تمر بها الى مسار آخر فيجعلك تتفكر فيها وتتفكر في الفوائد التي حصلت عليها ... يساعدك على تجاوزها بدون أن تترك أثرها عليك ....فالتفكر يحدد تفاعلك مع الأزمه التي ربما لها أكثر من حل ... وربما هي لاتستحق منك كل هذا العواطف المهدرة .

فهو يركز تفكيرك على هدفك .. والدروس المستفاده .... وملاحظه الخيارات الأخرى المتاحه أمامك .

التفكر يجعلك تفكر بالخلق والخالق ... وتساعدك على أن تضع الأمور في ميزانها الحقيقي سواء كانت دنيويه أو روحانيه .

إنه فضـــــاء واسع لمن أراد ان يلج فيه ...

والتفكر يختلف عن القلق ....القلق يجهد الفكر والبدن ...أما التفكر فهو يتفكر في الأسباب والنتائج وكيفيه تجاوز الأزمه .. وهل تستحق مني كل هذا أم لا ... وستجد نفسك بعد جلسه التفكر نشيط النفس .. كأنك فلت من عقال وستواصل مسيرة حياتك وستواصل حياتك من إنجاز الى إنجاز لأنك حصلت على العلم بالتفكر ...لا بالتجربه مرة ثانيه ...يقول المثل (لا أحد يتعلم إلا من كيسه أي من تجربته) لكن التفكر يمنحك فرصه التعلم بدون أن تجرب في الواقع وبدون أن تتعرض لهذه الصدمه أو هذه العقبه لأنك حصلت على العلم بالتفكر . فأنظر على جمال هذه الأداة .

بعكس القلق الذي يجعلك مقيد الى هذه المشكله أو العقبه التي تواجه مسيرك .وربما يوقفك تماماً.

(4-1) التــــفكّر و هــــدف من نوع خاص :-

التأمل سوف يساعدك على التفكير أو يطرح سؤال (لماذا أنت هنا؟)

يساعد على وجود تلك الرغبة بوضع بصماتك في هذه الحياة.

يساعدك على إعداد نية فقط النيه للقيام بشيء قبل أن تغادر هذه الحياة تعتز به.

فقط إضمار نية صادقه أنك تريد أن تكون في خدمة ذلك الكون العظيم كافي ..لأن تضع إسمك بين أسماء أناس عظماء أصبحوا عظماء بنواياهم أولاً ومن ثم نواياهم قادتهم لتحقيق افعالهم العظيمة ..... الله عز وجل سوف يهديك و سوف يساعدك على تحقيق هذا الهدف الخاص.

إنه هدف من نوع خاص ... أنت قد لاتعرف كيف يمكن أن تكون في خدمه هذا الكون .... أنا متأكده أن أغلبكم ربما يضحك ويقول أنا بالكاد أعرف ماهي أهدافي

وأنا أقول لك وأنا أيضا مثلكم ... ولكن التأمل ينقل تفكيرك الى مستوى أعلى ... يجعلك ترغب في فعل شئ ما له تأثيره

بصراحه أقول لكم أنني كنت يوماً مثلكم الى أن كانت حياتي معرضه للخطر بسبب الحرب ..وشعرت ان النهاية أزفت لامحالة .... وكنت خائفه جداً وهنا طرح هذا التساؤل ...

كل الناس ستغادر يوماً هذه الحياة ... لا أحد يخلد فيها .. وأحسست أني قد أغادر الحياة مثلما قدمت اليها .. لم اضف شيئاً اليها.

وتمنيت صدقاً يومها أن يساعدني الله ويحفظني .. ويعطيني الحياة ... ويعطيني القدرة على فعل شئ ما .. فإذا حان وقت رحيلي أكون سعيده بما أنجزت ...

لن أنسى هذا التفكير الذي كان يراودني كلما ادلهم الخطب ..

فأنا مثلكم لا اعرف ماذا يمكنني أن أفعل لهذا العالم .. ولكني افعل ماأستطيع في حياتي الخاصه .. البسيطه جداً ... أحاول تحقيق أهدافي الخاصه .التي لاتتجاوز ....اصلاح بيتي (بيتي) وإصلاح حياتي .... وأما الهدف الكبير والذي غالبا ما يراودني ... لا أستطيع حتى أن اسميه هدف بقدر ماأسميه رغبه .. في أن أمتلك القدرة على فعل شئ يستحق الذكر في هذه الحياة

ربما تكون نوعاً من الفلسفه ... ولكنها من أرقى الأفكار التي ممكن أن تنقلك الى مستوى آخر ... فتجد إهتماماتك قد إختلفت .

وتشعر دوماً أنك تبحث وتبحث عما تستطيع فعله .

(4-2) إسكات الأفكار :-

بما أننا نتكلم عن التفكّر .. لابد أن نتكلم عن أسكات الأفكار ... أو نستطيع تسميته علم إسكات الأفكار ..أو عدم الانجراف بالمحيط . بصراحة قد احترت بوضع هذا الموضوع مع جلب البهجة والسعادة المباحة الى حياتك ... أو مع إدارة الوقت وتنظيمه ... ولكني فضلت أن أذكره هنا كملحق بالتفكّر .. لأنه تابع للتفكّر ..ولأنه نوع من قيادة الفكر والذات ... فإذا قدت فكرك وذاتك استطعت قيادة حياتك الى ماتريد وتطمح بسهولة ويسر .. وستنعم براحة البال والسلاسة في حياتك ... وستبثها الى حياة الاخرين ايضاً .

ماذا تقصدين بإسكات الأفكار بينما أنت تتحدثين عن التفكر وعن الاهداف ... ؟!

من المهم لمن كان له هدف معين ان يعرف كيف يسيطر على عواطفه وانفعالاته وحزنه وغضبه .. وهذا يكون اسهل بالبعد عن من يقوي هذه الفكرة .. او تلك في رأسي .. سواء كان هذا اشخاص .. او اسلوب حياة .

لابد من التفريق بين التفكّر وإسكات الأفكار .. سبق وأن قلنا أن الفكر قوة عظيمة .. والسيطرة عليها من أهم التمارين التي يمكنك القيام بها.

إسكات الأفكار يساعدك على السيطرة على فكرك وعلى الخروج من دوامة قد تقع فيها.. وليس لها مخرج .. قد يكون جلب البهجة والسعادة المباحة والإندماج في محيطك يساعدك نوعاً ما على إشغال فكرك بعيداً عن المسألة التي تشغل تفكيرك .. لكن إسكات فكرك بنفسك هو شئ في غايه الدقة .. لأنك تحتاجه بشدة في حياتك .

إسكات الأفكار يعطيك مرونه عاليه في التفاعل مع مجريات الحياة .. ويعطيك زمام الأمور فتكون تحت سيطرتك خياراتك أنت ...

كمن يفكر في قوت يومه ولا يتجاوزه الى الغد .. فهذا نوع من اسكات الافكار .. ونوع من القوة .. ونوع من السعادة وهداة البال بنفس الوقت يعطيك مساحة خالية .. يوسع المدى حولك .

هو نوع من الرضا ... أو هو نوع من المرونة العاليه والقوة العاليه .. فأنت بإسكات أفكارك لاتذوب في الآخر تماماً .. لاتختفي .. أنت موجود لكنك ... مراقِب ..المراقبه تعطيك فرصة أن تكون على الحياد .

والحياد من أجمل الأشياء التي تساعدك على إتخاذ قرار بالمواصلة .. بإسكات الأفكار انت لديك مساحة واسعه من الخيارات ... مساحة واسعه من التغيير دون فقدان ذاتك . ... وأهدافك .

ليس كل شخص يمتلك مهارة إسكات أفكاره .. فالكثير بل معظم الناس تضيع أو تسيطر عليها مشكلة معينة أو حالة معينة ... أو حتى فكرة معينة ... ولايستطيع الخروج منها ... بل هناك من لايفكر أساساً بالخروج منها لأنه يعتبرها من سياق حياته .

التفكّر من جهة .. وإسكات الأفكار من جهة أخرى .. لابد لك من تخصيص وقت معين للتفكّر بالجلوس في مكان هادئ .. وبعيد عن الضجيج .. وتخصيص وقت معين لهذه الفترة .. تتفكر فيها فيما فعلت وماهي الأخطاء التي وقعت فيها مثلاً .. وكيف يمكنني تلافي هذه الأخطاء .. أو أتفكر في شئ كان من الصواب فعله .. وماهي أهميته .. أو أتفكر في حياتي ومجرياتها مثلاً .

و إسكات الأفكار من جهة أخرى لابد لك منها .. فلابد من تخصيص وقت معين أحاول فيها أن أسكت أفكاري .. والغي فيها إحساسي أو أسيطر فيها على أحساسي ..

هذه الحالة تساعدك على الخروج من دائرة المضمار الذي أنت فيه .. لتنظر بوضوح أكثر الى حياتك أو الى الموضوع الذي تعيشه .. أو الى الطريق الذي تسير فيه بإتجاه هدفك .. هل هذا هو الطريق الصحيح أم لا ؟!

هل يناسبني أم لا .. وهكذا

سكوت الأفكار مهارة ... فقد تقرأ ... أو قد تمارس الرياضة ... أو قد تستمع الى تلاوة من القرآن الكريم بإنصات وتمعن .. أو قد تستمع الى الموسيقى .. أو قد ترسم ... أو قد تمارس رياضة اليوغى ... أو تمارس الرسم .. أو حفظ القرآن ...

أو حفظ الأبيات الشعرية ..

والكثير الكثير من النشاطات التي ستجد نفسك تبتكرها .. لإسكات أفكارك والخروج من حالة الإندماج السلبي في معضلتك أو في دوامة الحياة .. أو في سعيك لهدفك

بل قد تجد أن الحياة زاخرة بالأهداف .... فأنت غير مقيد بهدف واحد .. إسكات الأفكار يعطيك هذا الحيز وهذا الميدان الواسع ... وستجد أن تعلقك بهدف واحد .. تعلق آمالك عليه .. وتكرس جهدك ووقتك له في غير مجدٍ في الوقت الحالي .. لذلك ستجد نفسك تنغمس بأهداف أخرى .. بنفس الأهميه .. مع احتفاظك بالهدف الأول ...

وهذا مايجعل إنجازاتك متجددة .. وهذا مايجعلك بعيداً عن اليأس .. بعيداً عن الإحباط ...

الذي لايتفكّر .. ولايمتلك مهارة إسكات أفكاره .. سيكون مثل الذي يتخبط في الرمال المتحركه .. كلما تحرك زاد غرقه فيها .. وهكذا مشكلات الحياة أحيانا .. أو هكذا من يمر بشعور معين يسيطر عليه تماماً .. فهذا الشخص كلما زاد أنغماسه في هذا الشعور زاد بعده عن الحقيقة والصواب ..

لذلك لابد لك من الحفاظ على نفسك قريباً من بر الأمان ... قريباً من الحياديه .. والرضا .. والقبول ... والمواصلة ...

أن تحافظ على رباطة جأشك .. تحافظ على هدوءك وسكينتك .. إذن انت قوي .

والحقيقة أن هذا له أصل في ثقافتنا نحن ,,, وله أصل عند علمائنا الأفاضل .. فمثلاً يقال أنصتْ الى القرآن .. ولايقال استمع للقرآن .

أو يقال لاتعبد الله للذة الخشوع .. ولكن أعبده للعبادة .

أو يقال العمل عبادة ... لأن من يعمل يكون مشغول بعمله ... مسكت لأفكاره ... مع إرتباطه بمبدأه .. العبادة .. و تحري الحلال ...

الموضوع بسيط جداً لكنه في نفس الوقت عميق جداً .. .

في وقتنا الحالي تجد الكثير من الناس مرتبط بالسوشيال ميديا .. او بالتلفزيون والاعلام ... لذلك تجد الكثير من التطرف في المشاعر والأفكار .

تطرف في الحـــب .

تطرف في الديـــن .

تطرف في مشاعر الغضب .

تطرف في مشاعر الحـزن .

لأنه لايوجد عمل ... ولايوجد إنشغال حقيقي ... ومن جهة أخرى لايوجد هذا الوعي بمهارة إسكات الأفكار .. أو الخروج من دوامة الفكر العام او المحيط...

بالأحرى لايوجد هذه الثقافة لدينا ..... ثقافة إدارة الذات .... وادارة العواطف .. والحيادية (عدم التفاعل والانفعال)

إدارة الذات تكــون بإدارة الفكر
..والعاطفة .. والوقت

سهير الحســن

5-THE POWER OF THOUGHTS

We can call it (the power of thought) ... because it is a powerful force ... if you can afford to own and control it... You went forward

In the Islamic religion, for example ... of the acts of worship in which I mentioned... one of their practicing is a meditation,

For its importance in building strong minds ... so own this power... The power of think.

As well as those who live in places far from the hustle of life ... like those who live in villages... Or in places where there is no crowd ... And those who do not have a social activity intensive they practice meditation automatically and on a daily basis

They are far from random... And their thoughts are clear ... And their ability to figure out things is strong because of the clarity of mind, which they received by the continuous training on meditation

They have the power of thoughts automatically >>>

...

Here you are ... Another weapon... Of the most powerful weapons that help you to achieve your goal ... whatever it was........ Easily and smoothly

(The power of thoughts) or in other words... (Clarity of mind).

5- الريـــــــــاضـــة :-

قد يعتقد البعض انها مهمة من الناحية الصحية فقط .. او للرشاقة وجمال الاجسام ... فقط ... وقد يعلق قائلاً .. ليس لي حاجة لأكون رشيقاً .. وأما الصحة فهي من الله عز وجل .. والحمد لله على كل حال

وهذه من الاخطاء الشائعة جداً في مجتمعنا .. وانا هنا اجيب الرياضة مهمة ومهمة جداً لصاحب الطموح ... او لصاحب الهدف .. فهي تنــــــــــــظم طاقتك ... فالشخص الذي يمارس الرياضة لايكون انفعالي بل يكون هادئ لانه تخلص من معظم الطاقة الزائدة والمحبوسة في جسمه .. ومن جهة اخرى هي تعزز الثقة بالنفس بطريقة عجيبة ... وتساعد الشخص على اثبات ذاته . فنادرا ماترى من يمارس الرياضة فاقداً لثقته بنفسه .. او حزين .. او منفعل .. او منطوٍ..فتراه خفيف الظل .. خفيف الروح ... متنفسه الرياضة .. وبمرور الزمن وبعد ان يعتادها .. تشعر انه لديه شئ من الابداع .. لان الرياضة تساعد على التركيز .. تركيز الافكار وصفاءها .. وسهولتها .

الرياضة .. هذه الممارسة المنقرضة في اولوياتنا .. تعتبر الرياضة من اهم الممارسات اليومية التي قد تساعدك على التركيز اولاً فهي تخرجك من الروتين .. تخرجك من ان تكون نسخة مكررة ... تساعدك على ان تكون انت .. نفسك .... تساعدك على اسكات الافكار والتي سبق وان تكلمنا عنها ...

هي موجودة في سُنـة حبيبنا المصطفى صلى الله عليه وسلم ..واوصى بها للفتيان .. (علموا اولادكم الرماية والسباحة وركوب الخيل) فهذه من الرياضات التي تنقل الشخص من حال الى حال وكلنا نلاحظ الفرق في شخصية الفتى الذي يمارس رياضة ما وبين شخصية الفتى الذي لايمارس اي رياضة وفي رأيي لاغنى عنها .. كجزء من روتين الحياة اليومية ..

مهمة لجميع الاشخاص لكن لها اهمية خاصة للشخص الطموح .. ويسعى الى هدف ما ويصبو اليه .. يخطط له .. ويعمل بجدية للوصول اليه

ومع الاسف في مجتمعنا الشرقي (المرأة) اكثر من يفتقر الى مجال لممارسه الرياضة ... وهي من احق الاشخاص بتوفير هذه الوسيلة فهي ام وزوجة وربة بيت ... هي نصف المجتمع

فغالبا مانرى الزوج منهمك في عمله .. والمرأة هي من تخطط للأطفال .. تخطط للبيت وللتعليم وللنزه .. وتقريبا لكل شئ .. فهي تستحق من المجتمع ان يفكر في كيفيه توفير وسيلة تساعدها على التنفيس عن نفسها ... وعلى تركيز افكارها ... بالمفيد والمهم .. والاصلح للاولاد ..

فانصح بممارسة الرياضة للعائلة وللاطفال .. ولكل افراد المجتمع .. ولك شخص عنده طموح بشكل خاص .. فهي من وسائل المواصلة والصبر .. والعزيمة ...

6-THE SCIENCE:-

The second weapon that can helps you a lot to the achieve is The science... Science here does not mean the science of universities or schools ... But knowledge of everything linked to your goal ... Search... Ask... Check ... The more you know about your goal, the more you'll getting it faster and easier.

The easiest example to bring you the idea

When you want to get married ... the first thing ever you going to do is looking for the right person who you can start with him, build your family with him... even in any one know there is something call the time of engagement before to get marriage ... it's time to know your spouse ... so the more you know about him the more you can override the troubles later ..

Or if you want to start business the more you know about that business the more you can success in it

So planning ... and knowledge important for any goal that you want to get... The more you have acknowledge

The more your way to achieve was easier and faster. And to have the science or knowledge you have to be patient and calm and humbling for who you ask.... Humility for those who I ask from their knowledge... The arrogant does not benefit from science or advice, because its prevents him from using his knowledge and his ignorance, prevents his intelligence and stops him. So it's a very important thing from my point of view and from the point of view of the scientists who have already studied on their hands and from our experiences that we've been through that have taken from the days of our lives.

Humility for science ... We have already said the power of the thought ... you have to restrict this power with the constraint of science... The ancestors say science is a way. One of the righteous says that if you want the happiness of the world and the afterlife, then you should learn. (learn) The whole science is good ... humility... Ask... respect it. .. The words of those with knowledge did not come in vain. Our parents say (he learned only from his money) it's a person who insists in keep going through the trials without listening to those who are older than him or know more than him. If you doesn't learn from the teachers. Then the life going to teach you (life experiences). So save effort and time. And listen to the experiences of others.

Example:- emotional relationship. You're when you want to get married. You're automatically looking for someone that who you can spend the rest of life with him ... Easily... And if you find him, you study this personality, studying his thoughts and, ideas and objectives. There is even

6-العِـــــلْم :-

السلاح الثاني الذي يمكنك بسهولة من المسير في ركب الإنجاز وتحقيق الأهداف هو العِـــلْم ..نعم استطيع ان اسميه (سلاح) لقوته الفعالة .. فلايوجد اهداف ولاطموح ولا انجاز بدون العلم .. بدون العلم الانجاز يصبح خراب ... والتخطيط يصبح عبث ... والتقدم يكون تأخر وجهالة ... و العلم هنا لا أقصد به علم الجامعات أو المدارس ... وإنما العلم بكل شئ مرتبط بهدفك ...لذلك نقول (إبحث).. (إسأل).. (تحقق) .. (خطط) ... كلما كان علمك عن هدفك أوسع .. كلما كان طريق تحقيقه اسهل واسرع . ... والعلم هنا يحتاج الى صـــــبر ... وهدوء .. وسكينة ... وتواضع لمن اطلب منه العلم ... فالمتكبر لاينتفع بالعلم ولا بالنصيحة لان كبره يمنعه من ان يستخدم علمه وجهله يمنع ذكاءه ويوقفه ..

لذلـــــك من الاشياء المهمة جداً من وجهة نظري ومن وجهة نظر العلماء الذين سبق ان درسنا على ايديهم ومن تجاربنا التي مررنا بها والتي اخذت من ايام عمرنا

تواضع للعلم ... سبق وان قلنا الفكر قوة ... فقيد عنان هذه القوة بقيد العلم ... يقول السلف

العلم منـــــــجاة .. ويقول احد السلف اذا اردت سعادة الدنيا والاخرة فعليك بالعلم ...

والعلم كله خير ...

تواضع له .. اطلبه ... احتـــــرمه ... كلام من له علم لم يأت عبثاً ..

يقول ابائنا (لايتعلم الا من كيسه) على الشخص الذي يصر على ان يخوض غمار التجارب بدون ان يصغى لمن هم اكبر منه او اعلم منه .. فالذي لايعلمه المعلم .. تعلمه التجارب

فاختصر الطريق .. ووفر على نفسك الجهد والوقت .. واستمع لتجارب الاخرين او من له علم

واسهل مثال اوصل لك به الفكره

العلاقه العاطفيه .. أنت عندما تريد الإرتباط .. فإنك تلقائياً تبحث عن شخص تستطيع أن تقضي معه بقيه حياتك الى الأبد بسعاده .. بسهوله .

واذا وجدته تدرس هذا الشخص تدرس تصرفاته وأفكاره وأهدافه .. حتى أن هناك في جميع الاعراف شئ يدعى (فترة الخطوبه) فهي فترة العلم بهدفك ألا وهو شريك الحياة

كذلك إذا كان لديك مشروع ما ... فأنت تدرس هذا المشروع بشكل مفصّل .. وتعرف كل تفاصيله قبل البدء به هذه الدراسه توفر عليك الكثير من المال والجهد والوقت لتحقيق الإنجاز .. الا وهو نجاح هذا المشروع .

فغالبا المشاريع التي تبدأ بدون دراسه يكون مصيرها الفشل .

إذا كنت تريد بناء بيت لابد لك من استشارة مهندس مختص وأخذ رأيه لأنه صاحب علم بالبناء ...

something called (engagement period) it is the period of knowledge with your goal which is a life partner as well.

So you are about real step in your life and you going to put the base for your own family … and the earlier you start the earlier you will build your family and you are about going through in real life … and you going to gain new aim by the way.

In the other side you have another option …

Just going on with any relationship for fun and later you goanna surprise that every one of your friends have his own family and his own kids and his own job and maybe he made a money also beside his beautiful family.

So you are alone … without any accomplishment …

فالعلم هو الشئ الأساسي الذي يدفعك في الطريق الصحيح للحصول على ماتريد ... وينبهك لتلافي الأخطاء التي ممكن ان تقع فيها .

العلم هو المصباح الذي يضئ لك الطريق لتسير على هدى في طريق تحقيق ذاتك وطموحاتك ..

العلم مصاحب للنزاهة .. لذلك كان أي هدف مرتبط بالعلم ... هدف واضح المعالم ... هدف له اساس صحيح ... وبعيد عن العشوائيه ... وبعيد عن حب الظهور وعن كل مايشوش الصورة امامك .. فانت مركز ومتواضع ومخلص في نيتك وارادتك لمعرفة الصواب في هذه المسألة فتلغي ذاتك تماماً ,,, وتلغي غرورك فاذا الغيت غرورك وكبرك وغرورك ظهرت نزاهتك .. انت تريد فعلا الوصول .

لماذا العلم مرتبط بالنزاهة .. لأن الغير نزيه سوف يتبع طرق غير نزيهة ... الطرق الغير نزيهة تعني العشوائية .. والعشوائية تعني أن ماستحصل عليه زائف .. وزائل .. وغير مبارك ..

البعض قد يستهين بهذه الكلمة .. ولكنها عظيمة التأثير .. بل يمتد تأثيرها الى ماحولك ... ويحرف حتى أهدافك لتكون أهداف غير ذا فائدة مهما تعبت في الحصول عليها ..ومهما توقعت انها أهداف عظيمة ونبيلة .. بل يمكن التعبير عن ذلك بــ (الضياع في وسط الفوضى) لأن ماحولك قد يكون ملئ بالفوضى ... فالهدف النبيل لايتحقق بالسبل غير النزيهة .

تمسكك بالنزاهة والعلم يعني أنك على الطريق الصحيح في التمييز والإصرار ..على النجاح بطريقتك أنت ... كن أنت صاحب التأثير فيمن حولك .. لاتذوب في وسط الفوضى أو الجهــــــــل .. أو أنعدام النزاهة ...

فهذه ليس لصاحب الهمة العالية ... والطموح العالي ... الطموح العالي بالحصول على خيري الدنيا والآخرة ..

لا انعدام النزاهة ليست صالحة لاي صاحب هدف .. مهما كان الهدف يبدو صغيرا وغير مهم ..

هنا انت قد وصلت .. وامتلكت مفاتح تحقيق اهدافك .. بسهولة ويسر .. لا بل قد يمتك تأثيرك الى من حولك .. لان الشخص المثابر .. والطموح وصاحب الهمة العالية وصاحب الاخلاق الرفيعة .. طالب العلم والنزاهة يصبح ممن لهم تأثير في هذه الحياة .. وممن لهم بصمة في هذه الحياة .. قد يمتد تأثيرك الى مدى بعيد ان لا تتوقعه ..

كمن لايفتأ يذكر جده أو اباه .. ابي فعل وجدي كان يقول .. هؤلاء اشخاص لهم بصمة ولهم تأثير امتد عبر اجيال .. لم تأت اعتباطاً ..لقد فعلوا الكثير والكثير .

. ذكرنا في هذا الكتاب ضع بصمتك

كن أنت الخــــــير أينما حللــــت

كن كالغيث أينما حللت استبشر الناس وهلل . بنجاح يتبعه نجاح يتبه فلاح .

رب اجعلني مباركا اينما كنت

رب انزلني منزلاً مباركاً وانت خير المنزلين .

Each real step in your life leads to another one.

[Family ____ kids ____ money]

Jobs__ fun __ vacation

(Real life)

Suhair alhasan

If you have a project ... You're studying this project in detail. And you know all the details before you start. This study saves you a lot of money, effort and time to achieve. It is the success of this project. Most projects that start without study are doomed to failure.

If you want to build a house you must consult a competent engineer and take his opinion....

And so on in each step in your life... In each goal...

Just decide what is your goal and now you have all the tools that can help you to get that goal.

Science is the key that pushes you in the right way to get what you want... And alert you to avoid the mistakes that may fall in. Science is the lamp that lights you up to walk on the path to improve yourself and your ambitions.

Science is a companion to integrity. So any goal was related to science...

You can defined it clearly... A goal that has a valid basis ... And far from randomness ... And away from the showing off and from all the confusion of the picture in front of you. You are focused, humble and sincere in your intention and your willing to know the right way in this matter, so you completely canceling yourself, and cancel your ego, so if you cancel your pride and ego, your integrity will appear. You really want to get there. Why science is about integrity. Because dishonest people will follow unfair ways... Unfair way mean randomness. And randomness means what you're going to get is false. And a descendant. And unblessed. Some might underestimate that word. But it's very influential. Its impact extends to what is around you... And even distort your goals to be useless goals no matter how hard you get them. And no matter what you think, they're great and noble goals. This can even be expressed by "getting lost in randomness around you" because what is around you may be full of chaos...so the goal ... is to make a goodness and more important in your life

This is where you've arrived. And you've got the approaches to achieving your goals. Easy and smoothly

And here your influence may be go to your son or your family.' Because the one who's persistent. Ambitious, high-powered, high-moral. The student of science and integrity ... he is an influencer in this life. And those who have a fingerprint in this life. They are who made the happiness for themselves and for the others ... They are blessed people.

Your influence may extend to a long way that you don't expect.

It's like you when you remember your grandfather or father .you say my father did... He was great man... Those people have impact in this life... They worked hard to be... To help us to be whom we are now

So their impact exceed even their time ...

. These are the people who have a fingerprint and have an impact in this life.

153

BE ONE OF THE INFLUENCER IN THIS LIFE.

HAVE THE HONOR

Suhair alhasan

7-THE SO-CALLED (LET IT GO):-

this factor is so important if you want to going forward .. And shorten the way to your goal... and this factor used with knowledge.. This factor is considered a confusing factor in some way for those who do not understand it correctly... (let it go) that every human being can do it only if he has a real will to reach his goal... like the one who climbs the ladder, jumping up the stair two steps together. He needs the audacity, the will of determination and the will to continue, and I'm here talking about (let it go) I'm talking about the one who has. It is not for those who do not have ... Because scientists say. For those who don't. And this is for those who want to catch up with influencers in this life. Who have a fingerprint), and if you can't be ascetic, you are far from influencing, i mean, for example, I am unmarried and you answer (I don't want to get married) but you are planning to achieve... You are here far away from achieving!

Because it is not for those who do not have... And if you're in the late ranks, there's no new achievement for you. ... No achieve mean no influence.

You are in the same level that you start so

Define your goal ... then let decide what the things that I don't need for right now and let go!

Simply!

7-الـــزُهـــد أو مايسمى (بالتـخلي عن)

من الاسلحه الرائعه والتي لابد لك من امتلاكها اذا كنت تريد المسير قدماً في تحقيق الأهداف .. وإذا كنت تريد أن تختصر الوقت في الوصول الى هدفك هو سلاح أو عامل الزهد وهذا مع العلم يكون رائع التأثير :-

يعتبر هذا العامل عامل مربك بطريقة ما لمن لم يفهمه بطريقه صحيحة ...فالزهد هنا هو قـــوة لا يستطيع امتلاكها كل إنسان إلا إذا كانت لديه إراده حقيقيه في الوصول الى هدفه ... لإن مثله مثل الذي يرتقي السلم قفزاً درجتين درجتين او ثلاثه ثلاثه معاً .

فهو يحتاج الى جرأة .وإرادة عزيمة ومواصلة وأنا هنا اتكلم عن الزهد للذي يملك .. وليس للذي لايملك ... لان العلماء يقولون ..(لازهد لمن لايملك) .. وهذه لمن يريد ان يلحق بركب المؤثرين بهذه الحياة ..الذين لهم بصمة .اذا كنت لاتملك .. فلا تدعي الزهد واذا كنت لاتستطيع الزهد فانت بعيد عن التأثير

يعني مثلا انا غير متزوج

يجيبك (والله انا انا لا اريد الزواج) لاني اخطط لهدف ما ...

انت هنا بعيد كل البعد عن الانجاز

لانه لازهد لمن لايملك ... واذا كنت في الصفوف المتأخرة فلا انجاز جديد لك .. انت سوف تقبع في نفس المستوى الذي انت عليه وان كان مستواك الان جيد .. ولكن للطموح الذي يريد ان يمضي قدماً يجب ان تخوض غمار هذه التجربة لتكون مثل اقرانك .. فالاهداف هنا بخدمة الحياة والحياة الافضل .. والحياة الافضل تكون بكل ماهو طبيعي وسلس

فالزهد قرار .. ماذا احتاج هنا .. ومالذي لا احتاجه ومن ثم تتخلى عن كل شئ لاتحتاجه حاليا .. أو التي تربك مسيرتك ... في سبيل هدفك . أو التي لاتتناسب وطموحك أو هدفك

أعرف ان المعنى قد يكون صعب بعض الشئ على الكثير منا ... لكنه معنى عميق .. الخطوات الواسعه باتجاه الهدف .. تتحقق .. بهذا العامل لو عرف الإنسان الطموح استخدامه بصورة صحيحه ...

انا ضد من يقول انا اوقف حياتي وأتخلى عن كل شئ وأركز في الهدف ... وهذا هو الزهد

وأنا اقول لك أنك هنا بعيـــــــــــــد كل البعد عن تـــحقيق الهدف .... لابل أنت توقف حياتك .. ولا أجد للزهد أي مكان هنا .. .

هل سمعت المقوله (لاتضع البيض في سلة واحدة) ....؟

هذه المقولة تنطبق عليك عندما توقف حياتك في سبيل هدفك المزعوم .. وفي إعتقادي نادر جداً هم من يصلون الى أهدافهم بهذه الطريقه ...

لايجوز ان توقف حياتك وإعتبار كل شئ متعلقات .ماعدا هدفك . أنت هنا تخلط الأوراق . وتضييع على نفسك فرص عظيمه ...وتتعب نفسك .. تجهدها .. تحصرها في ميدان ضيق ... بينما الأصل هو السعه .. والأنطلاق .. والبهجه ... والخيارات المتعدده ... حتى أن بعض المتعلقات تجلب السعاده وتزيدك قوة الى قوتك

إنما الزهد يكون لبعض الخيارات المعينه التي تحتاج الى **شجاعه ورؤيه** لأتخاذها

مثلاً بعض العلاقات ... بعض الاشخاص يشغلك ويشغل عواطفك بينما أنت تعرف أنك لاتتوافق معه .. وقد بذلت كل جهدك لإصلاح هذه العلاقه ووضعها في المسار الصحيح ... دون جدوى .

فإتخاذ القرار بقطع هذه العلاقه يحتاج شجاعه .. لإنك تكون قد تعلقت بهذا الشخص ..وتعودت عليه .. بينما البقاء معه سيجرك الى طريق آخر بعيد عن هدفك الا وهو تحقيق الاسرة الدافئة التي تبني مستقبلها سوياً وتطمح لتنشئة اولادها النشئة الصحيحة .. فالمستقبل واضح امامك .. اسرة ... اولاد ... وفرة مادية .. مستوى معيشي معين .. استقرار .. عيشة هنية ... رحلات وسفر او حج ..فأنت تخطط لمستقبل مريح دنيوي واخروي في نفس الوقت .. فهو من انبل واعظم الاهداف الشائعة ... ان اخطط ان احسن وضعي المادي والاسري لاسرتي ولاساعد والدي على الحج فهنا الهدف متشابك ومتفرع وواضح امامك .. سبحان الله .. فهنا عندما تزهد احيانا بشخص انت تحبه ولكنك تعلم انك لن تحقق اي هدف مما سبق ببقاءك معه لانه غير مناسب .. فهنا الزهد يحتاج منك الكثير من الشجاعة والجرأة ووضوح الرؤيا .

وأنت هنا تخاف من الوحده .. وتخاف من البقاء دون رفيق لفترة ... وربما لاتجد شخصاً آخر يسد هذا الفراغ الذي سيتركه الاول .. وازيد على ذلك ربما سيقاطعك اهلك لانك تركت رفيقك او الشخص المخطط لان ترتبط به .. هم لايفهمون اصرارك ولايعرفون وضوح رؤيتك ...

هذا القرار صعب ... ولو تذكرت انني ذكرت في بدايه الكتاب .. (لايجب ان تخاف من الوحده والإنعزال) ... وهذه هي إحدى الأشياء التي تحتاج الى شجاعه .. ورؤيه واضحه ... (هل هذا الشخص يناسبني أم لا)

الموضوع شائك بعض الشئ ... لذلك كانت قوة التفكير ....(التفكــــــــر) .. و(الزهد) ..و(العلم) مرتبطه ببعض نوعا ما

فهذا الارتباط يعطيك الثقة بالنفس اللازمة لتحمل العواقب مهما كانت في سبيل المضي لتحقيق ماتطمح اليه .

وقد يكون في هذا المثال .... علاقه ناضجه . وحب صادق يستمر مدى الحياة ..تحصل به على الاستقرار العاطفي الذي يساعدك على الانجاز في المستقبل من الناحيه الماديه والمعنويه .

فكلما كان القرار قطعي وسريع في قطع العلاقه التي تعيق تقدمك .. كنت أسرع في المضي في المضي قدماً ... وأأكد أنه يجب أن تكون متمتع بالعلم الكافي .. والرؤيه الواضحه لما تريد .. لكي تتخذ هذا القرار ... فليس كل من يهدم اي علاقه لاتروق له هو صاحب طموح

الموضوع يحتاج الى حصافه نوعا ما.

مثال آخر :- شخص يعمل بعمل لايمت بصله لطموحه ... دخله ضعيف ... ليس فيه تقدم على الاطلاق ... هنا المكوث في هذا العمل نوع من الجمود .. وقد يؤدي به الى ان يظل طوال حياته في نفس المكان .

قرار ترك هذا العمل يعتبر مجازفه للكثيرين ... لكن ليس للجسور .. الذي لايخاف العقبات والصعوبات .. المندفع الى هدفه بدافع العلم والتخطيط .. والثقه بالنفس .

فهذا لايخاف من الضياع .. وان كان كل من حوله يحاول اقناعه بالعكس ..

هو لديه رؤيه .... هو لديه هدف يريد تحقيقه .

هو يفكر في نفسه ويفكر في عائلته ومن حوله ... لأنه بانتقاله لمستوى اعلى سيساعد نفسه وغيره .. فتراه ملتزم بهذا الهدف .. مُــصِــر عليه .... وهذه المثال على بساطته الا انه يعتبر من أكثر المواقف شيوعاً في المجتمع .. فهومن أكثر الصعوبات التي تقابل الأشخاص في حياتهم

قرار ترك عمل غير مناسب أو قطع علاقه غير ملائمه للمستقبل تعتبر من القرارات المصيريه للشخص الذي يكون في هذا الموقف .. وتأخذ الكثير من الشخص عاطفته وتفكيره .. ووقته ليستطيع إتخاذها ..

هنا انت امتلكت مفاتيح او ادوات تحقيق الاهداف

وليس لنا غنى عن الصلاة وطلب المعونه من الرب في هذه المواقف الصعبه

أتمـــــــنى للجميع أن يحققوا أهدافهم .. وأن يكون هذا الكتاب شئ ساعدك على إمتلاك رؤيه .. وتحديد هدف .. وأن يساعدك على إحراز إنجازات في الحيـــاة تفتخر بها

وتعتـز بها ..

أتمنى أن يكون كتابي هذا قد فتح لك الآفاق لتنطلق في الحياة .. وتنهل من وفرتها .. .

شكـــــراً لكـــــم

8-SPORTS

Some might think it's-important only for your health. Or for agility and body beauty...

And this is one of the most common mistakes in our society. I am here to bring sport to a very important and important task for the ambitious... Or the target. It regulates your energy ... A person who do the exercises is not edgy, but he is calm because he has rid himself of most of the excess energy trapped in his body.

On the other hand, it promotes self-confidence in another way... And help the person prove himself. You rarely see a sports man lose his self-confidence. Or sad. Or edgy... you can feel him Light spirit ... He can breathe by sports, and after he gets used to it. You feel like he's got a little creative. Because sports help focus. The focus and. And its ease.

Sports. This extinct practice from our priority. Sport is one of the most important daily practices that can help you focus first as it takes you out of the routine. Get you out of being a duplicate ... It helps you be you. (Yourself).... Help you to silence the thoughts that we have already talked about...

It is mentioned in our Sunnah of our beloved Mustafa (peace be upon him). He recommend it to the young boys. He ﷺ says teach your boys Swimming, archery and riding horse

It was the sports in his time ﷺ

The sports can transports the person from level to the next and we all notice the difference in the personality of the boy who exercises a sport and the personality of the boy who does not practice any sport and in my opinion it is indispensable. As part of the routine of everyday life. It's important for everyone, but it's of special importance to the person who have an ambitious.

I recommend the sports for family and children. And for all the members of the community. And anyone have ambition. .. It's means of continuity and patience. And determination your thoughts...

The book is finish

Hope that you like ... and hope that you enjoy it

And wish that this book can help you to walk forward... And get what you want to ... and make life full of happiness and abundance and life

شــــــــكرا لكم

Printed in the United States
By Bookmasters